Attacking
Modern Defenses
with
Belly Option Football

Al Black and Bill Manlove

Parker Publishing Company, Inc.

West Nyack, New York

Library of Congress Cataloging in Publication Data

Black, Al
  Attacking modern defenses with belly option
football.

  Includes index.
  1. Football—Offense. 2. Football—Coaching.
I. Manlove, Bill. II. Title.
GV951.8.B57 1985   796.332′2   84-26464

ISBN 0-13-050188-3

I am honored to dedicate this book to my beloved and indispensable wife Edna, the real "head coach," and to my tremendous family: my mother Viola; my daughter Kathy Fitzpatrick, her husband Jim, and their daughter Erin; my daughter Susan Collins and her husband Dan, and their sons Pat and Pete; and my daughter Nancy. Their lives have all been permanently (and I hope positively) affected by football.

Bill Manlove

This book is dedicated to my mother, Alice Black, who has supported my many endeavors.

Allen Black

What This Book Offers You

BELLY OPTION FOOTBALL has been around for over 30 years. We started using it during the 1960s, made revisions, and have had great success. Since then we have lived and died with the belly attack, while constantly revising it and adding new wrinkles to keep ahead of the latest defensive trends. We have also adopted successful concepts of the wishbone and veer attacks to our system of offense.

Both of our schools have used the belly offense exclusively and each of our teams has achieved success using different approaches in adjustments and innovations. This guide explains the various techniques we have used to combat the changing defensive trends of the last 15 years and outlines our most successful techniques against the newest defensive ideas.

Through the years we have developed two different, yet compatible, adjustment philosophies. Through the use of multiple blocking schemes and multiple formations, and aided by the simplicity of the belly option, we have been able to keep ahead of new defensive innovations. The versatile mix of these two concepts has enabled the belly attack to remain a potent offensive weapon throughout the multiple option era. This book offers a complete offensive strategy and a simplified game plan that is easily adapted to new circumstances week after week and year after year.

After years of researching the various forms of option football, we have developed a devastating play-action passing game with many variations that are easy to learn, yet new and flexible from game to game. Through experimentation, we have added a variety of counters that any option coach will find interesting and useful.

Because of our dedication to option football we have developed plans that permit us to attack alternately the linebackers, perimeter, or the down interior people with the running game. No matter how you wish to attack an opponent, the belly option has a formula that can achieve success. We have developed an isolation theory that lets you establish three-on-two, two-on-one, or two-on-zero option relationships at the corner.

You can use this book in preparation for every game. We have divided the book by defenses for the running game and secondary coverages for the passing game. In each area we offer several successful methods of attack. You will find something here that can help you diversify your attack every week.

We have also come up with an organizational format that will enable you to teach, motivate, and tactically use these new trends in your weekly game plan.

Al Black and Bill Manlove

Acknowledgments

This book would not have been possible without the excellent coaches who have worked on our respective staffs over the years. Their labors, expertise, and input have contributed greatly to our knowledge of the offense.

Also, many of the top coaches in the country honed our thinking, as did the defensive staffs of our opponents, who forced us to adjust week after week during our careers.

The players we have had the privilege to coach carried out our plans and in so doing helped immensely to lead the offense to where it is today.

To Peg Boyles, who struggled through our scribbling and scrawls to prepare our manuscript, we owe a very special thanks.

Contents

What Is
Belly Option Football?

*The one thing we learn from history is,
we never learn from history.*

Hegel, *Philosophy of History, 1832*

WHEN HISTORIANS EXAMINE the great battles of military history, they find many instances where this quote must have haunted those generals who didn't heed the mistakes of their predecessors. In 1863, during the pivotal battle at Gettysburg of the American Civil War, the fate of the Confederacy was sealed when General George Pickett's assault on the center of the Union line failed. Later, during World War I, when the German offensive stalled in eastern France, they devised a plan to attack the center of the Allied defenses at Verdun. This assault was designed to wear down the French Resistance and bring about its collapse. Months later this plan failed, and the Allies retaliated with the same strategy at the same place. After nine months there were 750,000 casualties, while the front remained unchanged. In a war of attrition there is seldom a winner, unless one side has the unlimited players (oops!—reserves) needed to wear the opponent down.

The military comparisons can be easily applied to football, since football is essentially a game of warfare. In the above analogies there is a lesson for you, the football coach. Both battles were built on an offensive philosophy that can be summed up in such familiar football phrases as: "Let's run right at them and wear them down." "We'll show them who is in charge." "Let's destroy their will to fight." There is nothing wrong with this

1

approach if you have sufficient resources. But, as with the generals who learned the hard way, there may not be enough reserves to bring about a successful conclusion to this type of strategy.

On the other hand, General William Sherman in the same Civil War introduced a philosophy of battle on his march to the sea. It called for an attack over a broad front seeking a weak spot in the enemy's defenses. When the breakthrough was established, all available troops were poured through the hole; then they penetrated as deeply as their supplies permitted. In June of 1940, the Germans refined the concept when they took advantage of the potential of twentieth century technology and swept across western Europe in a matter of weeks. This method of attack is called "lightning war" or blitzkrieg.

This book is built around the blitzkrieg concept. You don't want to hammer at the enemy's strengths and get bogged down in a war of attrition. You want to attack his weakest point with everything available. Your desire is to penetrate his primary front at its weakest point with all of the force you can muster. Option football is the equivalent of the "lightning war." You want to attack along a broad front, but focus your scoring drive at the weakest point in the defense.

Chapter by chapter you will examine each defensive scheme, define its weakness, and prepare an immediate attack at that area. There is no need to waste valuable time probing if you can determine the weakest spot before the battle starts. As the weak areas are defined we will offer you various ways to break through the defenses.

WHY OPTION FOOTBALL?

Below the professional level, option football has proven to be the most effective way to move the ball and score on a regular basis. There are many forms of option football. With the proper use of personnel, each type can be a smashing success. The Houston veer is great for some teams and the wishbone for others. The split T was the mainstay of amateur football for 20 years. All have proven to be effective. We have found, over the long term, the belly attack provides the best of each of these systems. For example, there are 300 high schools in or near the Delaware Valley. Approximately a dozen schools use the belly option. Recently a top-rated high school in southern New Jersey ran the belly option offense and remained undefeated; in eastern Pennsylvania, the top-rated team accomplished the same feat. At the college level, Widener University went undefeated and won the National Championship in the NCAA Division III while running the belly option attack. We don't believe this phenomenon is an accident, but a proper use of personnel within a sound offensive system. This scheme of offense is fairly well-known, so we will not dwell at length on its basic principles. This book is devoted to using option football to obtain the optimum results against each type of defense.

WHAT IS BELLY OPTION FOOTBALL?

This high-scoring offense is a four-back attack with a split end. The two set backs can be in an I or split-back set, depending on the individual abilities of the two players. The heart of the attack is the option or dive threat, usually to the strong side, supplemented by a counter with the slotback coming back against the grain. See Diagrams 1–1 and 1–2.

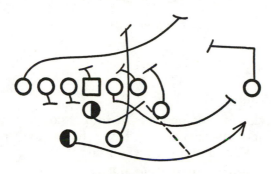

Diagram 1–1

Option Rules

One End—Second to inside off the line of scrimmage (LOS).

On Tackle—Block man on guard or onside linebacker (LB).

On Guard—Pull to running lane. Block first defender to show on running lane after you have made the turn upfield. Belly to 4 yards in backfield on first four steps.

Center—Show pass by stepping to front side, gap first.

Off Guard—If covered by a LB, fold to him around the center; if not, pass protect.

Off Tackle—Pass protect.

Off End/Off Slot—Clear LB and get to running lane and lead block.

Fullback—Fake over tackle's inside leg, then block free safety if you are not tackled.

Tight End or Slotback—Block a linebacker (LB) aligned over near tackle; if none, block inside on LOS.

Note: If onside tackle can't release to the LB, he can switch assignments with you.

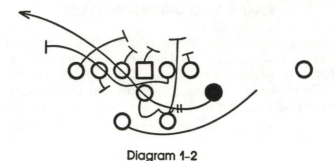

Diagram 1-2

Scissors Rules

Split End—Safety.

Offside Tackle—If a defender is in your inside gap, pull and lead through point of attack and block first defender to threaten running lane; area block from inside, over, outside.

Off Guard—Outside gap; if none, follow same rule as offside tackle's pull rule.

Center—Man over, lineman outside to side slotback (SB) aligns, or LB to same side.

On Guard—Inside gap; man over; show pass 1 count, then lead on running lane looking outside first.

On Tackle—Same as on guard.

On End—Inside LB, if none, turn near end outside.

There are three different fullback dives: the straight-belly, the cutback, and the outside veer. See Diagram 1-3. The option series can be run to the weak side, but we will usually run a counteroption to the weak side when the defense so dictates. See Diagram 1-4. The weakside attack is not a staple of the offense, but it must be kept handy for the opponent that uses an overshift to the strong side. The passing game is mostly play action and consists of three basic unit pass patterns that are the basis for all variations needed to defeat the various defensive schemes. See Diagrams 1-5, 1-6, and 1-7.

The most exciting aspect of this explosive offense is in the versatility of the blocking schemes. The blockers are seldom asked to muscle an opponent to complete their assignments successfully. Most of the blocks are screens or influence blocks. The opponent will seldom get bruised, but he will often be frustrated. After using this attack for many seasons, we have found it is not necessary to have a great running quarterback; also, the linemen need not be physically impressive for the offense to be explosive.

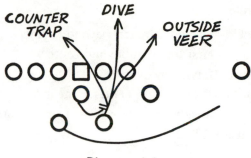

Diagram 1-3

Outside Veer Rules

On End—High block near deep third responsibility.

On Tackle—Block man on guard or onside LB.

On Guard—Block man in far gap or over center or inside LB.

Center—Out to offside guard, offside LB, or man over.

Offside Guard—Pull and seal through point of attack.

Offside Tackle—Front gap; pass block man over, or get to running lane and lead block.

Offside End—Get to running lane and lead block.

Tight End/Slotback—Same as option.

Diveback—After third step, veer to outside leg of the tackle's block.

Cutback Trap Rules

See counter trap. Trap is blocked same for both cutback and counter.

Dive Rules

Onside End—Same as veer.

Onside Tackle—Same as veer.

Onside Guard—Trap first beyond point of attack.

Center—Frontside gap; man over; backside LB.

Offside Guard—Frontside gap; pass block man over; if none, get into running lane.

Offside Tackle—Same as guard.

Offside End or Slotback—block safety.

Slotback/On End—Same as option.

Notes: Vs. "Odd"—defense change to man-for-man blocking.

Vs. "Gap"—(In onside guard-center gap) use isolation dive rule.

Isolation Dive Rules

Onside Tackle—Second lineman beyond center.

Onside Guard—First lineman beyond center.

Center—First defender to offside.

Offside Guard—Fold around center to near LB.

Offside Tackle—Inside gap; man over; man to outside.

Slotback—Inside LB.

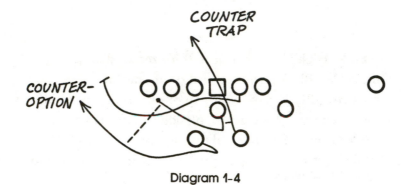

Diagram 1-4

Counter Trap Rules

Off End—Safety.

Off Tackle—Inside gap, show pass.

Off Guard—Pull and trap first to show past center.

Center—Offside gap on or off LOS.

On Guard—Block down to inside on or off LOS.

On Tackle—Block first LB from center out.

On End/On Slot—near LB.

Diveback—Read block on frontside LB and cut accordingly.

Counteroption Rules

Off End—Safety.

Off Tackle—Seal inside gap; show pass.

Offside Guard—Pull shallow for two steps, then get depth and lead to running lane. Same responsibilities as the option once you make the turn upfield.

Center—Over, backside gap.

Onside Guard—Number 1 defender to your side.

Onside Tackle—Number 2 defender to your side.

Onside End—Release and bump man with contain responsibility, then wall off near safety.

Fullback—Steps same as trap. Key offside LB and cut off his pursuit to pitch lane.

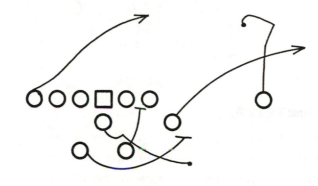

Diagram 1-5

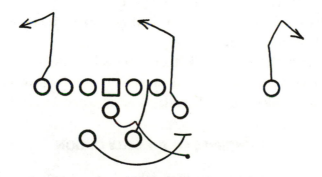

Diagram 1-6

Sprint Pass Block Rules

Onside Tackle—Inside, over, outside aggressive.

Onside Guard—Pull and seal onside end.

Center Offside/Guard/Offside Tackle—Onside gap aggressively; cup pass protection.

Fullback—Fill on frontside blitz; if none, run delay route.

Running Back—Seal up contain after faking option.

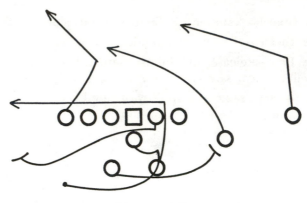

Diagram 1-7

Bootleg Pass Block Rules

Offside Tackle—Inside gap; cup pass protection.

Offside Guard—Pull same as counteroption and seal onside end.

Center—Off gap, cup protection to split-end side.

Onside Guard—First down lineman from center to outside.

Onside Tackle—second down lineman from center to outside.

Diveback—block first LB to show; if none, run drag under route.

Split End—Post pattern.

Tight End—Fake LB block, then run deep seam, out pattern.

Slotback—Fake down block then run 10 yard drag route.

Pitchback—Block backside end.

PRINCIPLES OF THE BELLY OPTION

Belly option football varies from other forms of option football in how the quarterback releases from the center. In the belly, the quarterback must get as deep into the backfield as possible on the first two steps. This is different from the veer quarterback, who works directly down the line in a style similar to the split T quarterback of the early 1950s. It also differs from the wishbone quarterback, who takes one deep balance step toward the fullback before starting the option.

The belly quarterback reverses as deep as possible into the backfield before starting the fullback ride. To help in this move, the diveback must align at a depth of 5 yards. The end result is a ride that develops slowly and requires the quarterback to come off the ride while advancing toward the line of scrimmage. This creates a totally different option read for the feather-technique defensive end, and forces that defender to abandon his normal techniques of defending the option. Once you get the defenders to play the techniques you want, the advantage goes to the offense. Diagram 1–8 shows the angle the quarterback uses as he approaches the line of scrimmage. Contemplate the read this gives the defensive end. Compare this to the quarterback's option angle on the other types of options (see Diagram 1–9). On the other options, the quarterback works toward the sideline; then he must plant and cut up into the hole vacated by the retreating end. Also, on other option series, the diveback either gets a flash fake or none at all. This move doesn't cause much hesitation as the defender continues his drift toward the sideline.

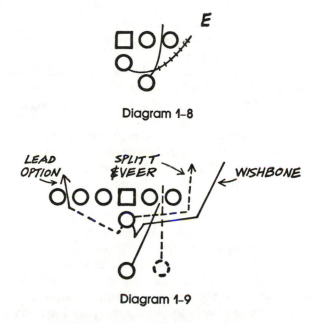

Diagram 1–8

Diagram 1–9

PHILOSOPHY OF BELLY OPTION FOOTBALL

This offense threatens the whole field until three steps after the snap of the ball. Every run and pass starts with the same action. Imagine the advantage of gaining a two-step head start on each play. It is the blitzkrieg theory: attack the opponent over a broad front, force him to spread out his defenses, and then martial your forces at the point designated for attack. Finesse is the key to making the belly option work properly. Show the ball at one spot, then have it reappear at another location. In addition to the option action the quarterback is always retreating into the backfield, setting up for a potential pass play.

The belly option is also based on the series principle, which is that every play in each series complements the others. The dive, option, and scissors look alike and each helps set up the other. In the counteroption series, the trap, option, and pass all develop off the same action.

To win consistently at the high school and college levels, a team must have a strong running game. Below the professional level, statistics do not favor the strong passing teams year after year. This trend might be changing in the Sunbelt, where the passers can work year-round to develop their throwing skills. But in most of the country the precision necessary for a strong dropback passing game is just not there. Though the belly option is a run-oriented attack, the passing game can be effective when it is used as a supplement to the running attack.

You want an offensive that has the potential to score at anytime from the base play of the series. With the belly option, the constant threat of the long-option run is always there. The fewest defenders are on the perimeter, and the focus of this offense is directed at that spot. Constantly running inside requires ball control; Ball control requires time, and time is always on the side of the defense.

The average length of our scoring drives at the high school level is 5.3 plays, and at the college level it is 6.2 plays. The average high school team cannot go more than an average of 7 plays without making a mistake, and the average college team cannot go more than 10 plays before an error stops them. A casual observation of the statistics shown here suggests that a ball control offense will defeat itself before it gets to the end zone. Our offensive statistics point out that when we score, it is usually done with the big play. Therefore, we are not trying to beat the odds each time we start an offensive drive.

To avoid errors, your offense must be kept simple enough so that it can always be mastered, but not so simple that it can be stereotyped. Offensive mistakes are more destructive than defensive aggressiveness. The defense must be kept off balance, while the offense is in complete mental control of its own actions. There are two ways to gain the advantage: through multiple offensive formations or with multiple blocking adjustments. If you can have two ways to block each play for every game or be able to change formations to gain the desired defensive adjustment, the offense is capable of maintaining the upper hand. When the offense is able to keep one step ahead of the defense, then your chance of making the big play is always imminent.

How you decide which method of attack to use is determined by your players' ability to handle the various approaches. Do you have intelligent linemen, intelligent backs, good speed, good technique, power in the backfield, or strength in the line? All of these factors must be evaluated before you can organize an attack that will defeat the defense. For example, when your linemen are capable of making line of scrimmage blocking adjustments, then that method can be stressed; when you have fast backs who can cut off straight-ahead blocks, you then have another method. By using the belly system, deception is the one constant that will help you beat the defense.

Each offense must be geared to the personnel at hand. Obviously, each offense gives a particular skill primary importance. This is the most important quality to a successful belly option attack. But if the fastest player you have is not a good athlete, don't complicate his responsibilities. He should catch only the pitch and run for the goal. With overall team speed you are able to diversify the attack. If the blocking talent is limited, you can flip–flop the players to take advantage of the skills of your best linemen.

The flexibility of this attack permits you to branch out in many directions without abandoning the basic principle of the offense. It is designed for adaptability and change so you can handle any situation that may be thrust at you and your players.

BELLY OPTION BACKFIELD TECHNIQUES

The following explanation is taken from Allen Black, *Modern Belly T Football* (West Nyack, NY: Parker Publishing Company, Inc., 1971).

Quarterback

On the outside belly we prefer the reverse pivot. It is easier for the quarterback to get depth into the backfield when he reverses out. We usually teach him the steps on a chalk line so he can more quickly visualize his footwork.

The first step on an option right is deep left. This step is to be as deep as possible and straight back, or at six o'clock. As he takes this step, he is to snap his head toward the fullback to locate the faking pocket. His second step with the right foot should be made directly at the fullback. This step should be taken while going away from the line of scrimmage, but it is an adjustment that is essential to create the meshing of the two. As he nears the fullback, he reaches back at arm's length and places the ball in the faking pocket.

At this point, while the quarterback is momentarily motionless, the ride begins. To extend the length of the ride as long as possible, the quarterback should take a balance step toward the dive hole with his left foot. When the fullback has gone beyond his reach, the ball is pulled out and the quarterback gains momentum by stepping with the right foot toward the offtackle hole. This step puts the quarterback in motion and gets him to move directly toward the inside of the defensive end. When the ball is removed from the fullback's pocket, it is brought directly to his chest and held tightly in both hands, so that it is in full view of the defensive end.

The quarterback is to maintain this 45-degree course toward the flag until he is attacked. Many times a crashing end will commit to the fullback's fake. In these instances the quarterback is to keep on the flag route until someone forces him to pitch. If the end goes for the running back, the quarterback will keep the ball looking to lateral later. If the end challenges the quarterback, he is to pitch the ball. The pitch is made with both hands in a basketball pass fashion; two hands from the chest stepping toward the pitchman. The lateral should be a dead-ball toss, rather than an end-over-end flip that is difficult to handle.

The quarterback is permitted no fancy faking—no fake pitches, fake steps, or head nods. If you teach your quarterback fancy fakes, bobs, and weaves, he may end up making multiple moves, but no progress toward the goal line. Too often you see the player making all the moves and going nowhere; fancy footwork merely wastes time. Your gauge to determine if the quarterback is pitching the ball at the right instant is to watch if he nearly gets tackled after he makes the toss. If he gets hit every time, then he is waiting too long. If he never gets hit, then he is pitching too soon.

Fullback

His feet should be 4½ yards from the line. His first step at the snap is on a 45-degree angle toward the dive hole with his near foot. His second step is to be directly at the guard–tackle seam. After this, he squares up to the hole and should run hard and low, making as big a faking pocket as possible. He is to try and make eye contact with the linebacker or the player with dive responsibility. He must be tackled on every play. When the quarterback removes the ball, he is to drop his outside shoulder and barrel into the dive hole. If the linebacker doesn't tackle him, he tries to intersect the free safety's angle of pursuit.

Running Back

When you run the option, your running back may line up either in the I or as the off halfback. If you don't have a fast running back, it's better to run this play from the I. The I enables a halfback with average speed to get in front of the quarterback for the option, but if this same back ran from a halfback position, he would not be able to reach the 45-degree angle necessary for a successful option.

If you run the option from the I, your running back must lose ground on his first four steps. The first step is an open step away from the line. As the back moves right, his next three steps (left, right, left) are away from the line. This retreat is necessary to keep the distance between him and the quarterback proportional, for the quarterback is reversing to a depth of 2 yards before he starts the option. After the fourth step the running back turns toward the flag and runs at a 45-degree angle to the sideline. If, for some reason, the quarterback does not immediately pitch the ball and is forced to make a cut in or out, the running back must also make a similar cut to keep the proper pitch depth and angle.

Train your running backs to catch the pitch in the same fashion they would catch a pass. They should catch it in both hands. They are to look the ball into the hands and not into the belly. The biggest problems occur when the running back is looking at the tacklers while the pitch is in the air. You can usually count on a fumble when this happens. After he catches the pitch, he is to continue on the same route, which is a 45-degree angle toward the sideline. The defensive halfback will be blocked by the pulling guard if he obstructs the track (running lane). When the guard commits on the block, the running back is to cut off his hat. This is the only cut you should expect the ballcarrier to make.

Pulling Guard

He is to pull deep and lead the pitchman. It is important that he pull deep for several reasons. If he pulls shallow, two things might happen that could cause the play to fail. First, he might get hung-up in the wash of blockers at the off-tackle hole. Second, a shallow pull would have him turning upfield far ahead of the running back, enabling the defender he blocks to recover and still be in time to make the tackle. A depth of 4 yards is sufficient enough to place him directly in front of the running back. When he crosses the line of scrimmage, he should be about 8 yards outside of the slotback and headed on a 45-degree angle toward the sideline.

In our scheme of football, we do not intend to overpower the opponent; therefore, we must be realistic in our approach to downfield blocking techniques. We want a block that is easily taught and easily executed. The running shoulder block provides us with this technique. We want our blocker to put his shoulder pad through the defender's belt, forcing the defender to come under control and use his hands to ward off the blocker. Thus, if our back is following close enough on the blocker's hip when the block is thrown, he will be able to break off the blocker's hat to daylight. This continuity of blocker and runner will not give the defender an opportunity to shed, recover, and still remain between the ballcarrier and the goal.

COUNTEROPTION BACKFIELD TECHNIQUES

Quarterback

Assuming the quarterback is straddling an imaginary line at the snap, he will step over that line as he reverse pivots to get to the side he is to option. His second step should be straight back along the same imaginary line. As he takes these steps the diveback will come as close to him as possible, passing over the spot where the foot of initial movement was located. After the open-handed fake or handoff to the diveback, he will pivot with both feet toward the off-tackle hole. As he makes the turn the ball is brought to the chest and the play develops exactly like the belly option.

Diveback

It is preferable that he align a step closer to the line on this action. On the snap, he should aim for the quarterback's foot farthest from the action of the option. When passing the quarterback, the diveback should make a good fake and cut off the block on the frontside linebacker. If he is blocking the offside linebacker, he should make the same move and start into the block on the seventh step downfield. This will place the fullback in good position to cut off the linebacker's angle of pursuit to the pitchman.

Pitchback

Since this is a slow-developing option, the pitchback must take a false step opposite the final action of the series, when he is aligned in the I formation. If he is aligned in split-backs, two false steps must be taken. After the turn around, the option develops the same as the belly option.

Pulling Guard

On the first three steps, he should pull as though he were going to trap. This will permit him to clear the quarterback and fullback fake. After this his pull should develop the same as it does on the belly option.

2

How to Dictate
Defensive Adjustments

FORCING THE DEFENSE to align in positions that are most advantageous to the offense is critical if a team wants to have consistent success moving the football. There are several ways you can manipulate the defense. By using each or all of unbalanced lines, multiple formations and motion defenses can be forced to adjust their personnel as the offense desires. Or, you can force the defense to stay close to their base alignment by always aligning in a double-tight formation with a wide receiver.

You must examine your personnel and determine which offensive method is best for your squad. If you are concerned with physical match-ups on game day, multiple formations, motion, and unbalanced lines are possible ways to provide the blockers with better blocking angles. If you fear confusion may result as the defense constantly changes alignments, then aligning in the basic formation and forcing the defense to do likewise might be the best thing to do.

BASE FORMATION PHILOSOPHY

When we speak of the base formation, we are referring to the formation shown in Diagram 2-1, with a tight end to one side and a slotback to the wide receiver's side. The remaining backs align balanced behind the quarterback, either split or in the I. By always showing this set, the defense is required to defend eight gaps, plus honor a wide receiver to the strong

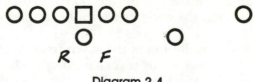

Diagram 2-1

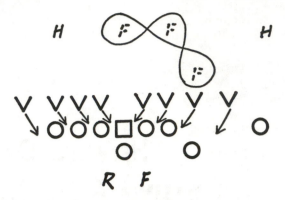

Diagram 2-2

side. If your opponents play an eight-man front, they must align their defensive front to protect those eight gaps along the offensive line. See Diagram 2-2. The secondary must respect the two ends with their half-backs, leaving only the free safety to play games. If they do anything else, the defense won't be sound. They may wish to play an overshift or do some stunting from their base defense, but when they violate the principles of that defensive scheme, weaknesses are created. When this happens the offense must be prepared to strike immediately.

When facing a seven-front opponent, the double-tight look forces the defense to align their front seven on the offense's front seven if they wish to remain sound to the principles of their particular defensive style. A defender must be aligned on the corner to contain the pitch out to the tight-end side. Another defender must be placed on the wide receiver. This leaves only the two safeties free to move around for adjustments and secondary stunts. By always showing the same look to the defense, the blockers can be fairly certain where they will find their blocking assignment. This saves teaching time and allows more time for the offensive line to get into blocking variations.

Option football is designed to create a constant threat at the perimeter of every defense. This is achieved when the offense gets that technical advantage on the perimeter by outnumbering the defenders at the point of attack. If the formation remains constantly tight, the defenders are locked into defending their individual gaps, permitting the quarterback to attack where the numerical advantage exists.

Another advantage of the base formation that aids the option quarterback as he tries to read the perimeter is in the simplicity of the option read.

The split-end set usually forces the seven-front defense to defend with an invert fill complimented by corner support to the tight-end side. When training the quarterback to run the option, you don't want him confused by too many reads. By forcing the defense to attack in the same manner each time, our quarterback finds it easy to pick up his reads.

Also, we are fairly certain that the defense will place the strongside contain (number 4) in a position that will take away the slant pass from the split end. This locks the defense into their basic alignment, making each block and the quarterback read more constant.

When the passing game develops off the same basic action, the offense has an additional advantage. The linebackers must honor the faking fullback before they can get into their pass drop. This permits the offense to have a simplified yet effective passing attack, because certain short zones will usually be filled late by defenders honoring the run fake.

Any time the defense violates their basic principles, the option attack has both the time and place to attack. This is the secret of the offense: look for the weakness presented, then attack. The defense should continue to align in a "book" alignment; then the option can always get the two-on-one or three-on-two perimeter advantage.

UNBALANCED LINE PHILOSOPHY

Using the unbalanced line is certainly not intended to be a way of life in the option offense, but a tactic that can always force the defense to move. The defenders can never dig in. They must always be looking to shift left or right. There is an unusual advantage here. Most adjustments are made by perimeter, but when facing an unbalanced line the interior must also adjust. The interior players are not usually aware of an unbalanced situation and must be told when and where to move. At this point communication becomes an integral part of successful defense. It is not unusual for a defense to adjust the interior the wrong way because an excited signal caller communicated poorly with his linemen. Obviously, when given enough time, most defenses will make a sound adjustment to the unbalanced line. But when they see it only occasionally and are forced to recognize it instantly, the advantage goes to the offense.

When facing an unbalanced line, the defender is forced to change his read. The nose guard is a good example. On an odd defense he always plays on the center, who seldom pulls. But, when shifted, he is required to align on a guard that is frequently pulling left and right. Instead of stepping to meet the charge of the man in front of him, he now must react to more angle blocks. These are small items, but require additional practice time. The more time you can require your opponent to spend reacting, the less time he spends acting.

Also, most teams treat an unbalanced line as an adjustment situation. Therefore, they are not as inclined to stunt when they see the unbalanced line, since they have already completed their stunt by adjusting to the new offensive alignment. This refers us back to the principal reasons for the double-tight formation, which suggest the defense will give you one basic alignment when they are in danger of becoming unsound.

Finally, if the opponent is threatening to overpower one of your linemen, you can get him to move elsewhere by going to the unbalanced line. This alone can save your linemen from some very long Saturday afternoons.

USING FORMATIONS TO NEUTRALIZE THE DEFENSE

By carefully selecting the right formation, the belly offense can dictate the type of pass coverages an opponent cannot play and at the same time gain a blocking advantage at the corner.

If a team likes to play man-for-man coverage and you feel that they would be easier to beat in zone, you can align in a double slot and use motion to get back to the I formation. Three deep man-for-man teams can be threatened with this alignment as shown in Diagram 2–3. Four deep teams can be challenged by aligning in an unbalanced trips look, then motioning back to the I, as shown in Diagram 2–4.

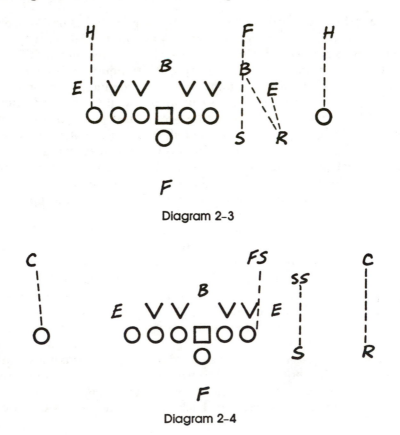

Diagram 2–3

Diagram 2–4

By moving either ends in or out, blocking angles can be established that will aid in the running of the option. If an eight-front team presents a problem at the corner, the split end can be brought in tight to the slotback to regain the lost leverage in the off-tackle hole. Inversely, if an opponent is in a seven-front defense and they like to sink their line when possible, and you feel that the offense will have better blocking angles when they use their maneuver, the tight end can be split to make the needed adjustment.

The slotback's alignment need not be planted in concrete, either. He is usually one of the smaller players in the belly option offense and is often given the job of blocking a much larger defender. He will have a better chance of completing his assignment if his alignment and attack positions are varied. If the slot aligns in a halfback set position, he sometimes gets a better block on a big tackle than if he tried to block down on him from the normal position, as shown in Diagrams 2–5a and 2–5b. Some defensive tackles react well to a down block when they see the offensive tackle going inside. But when he faces a halfback and fullback coming directly upfield to his inside and outside at once, he sometimes freezes, not knowing if he is to be sealed for the option or kicked for the dive. In other situations, a normal slotback flexed at 4 yards creates a problem for a 50 end, and a slot split 2 yards causes a problem for an eight-front tackle.

Any time you can cause doubt or force a defender to pause and think, the advantage passes to the offense.

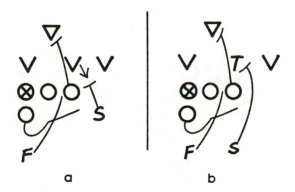

Diagram 2-5

USING MOTION TO OUTFLANK THE DEFENSE

Using motion to create a numerical advantage is achieved by the slot, running back, or either end. This is particularly effective against teams that like to play a monster defense and flip–flop their personnel. This style of defense is designed to take advantage of certain players' skills and hide the weaknesses of other players. Therefore, if you show strength one way and change it, you can attack the weakest area of the defense with the strongest part of your offense. If a team wishes to give a particular defender the pitch responsibility while another always covers the passing zone, you can use the end-in-motion to force them to switch that assignment. Diagram 2–6 shows a weakside option requiring the corner to cover the motion end (wingback technically) and the free safety filling on the option.

Motion can also be used with the wingslot formation to gain the advantages of both the wing and the slot. By deploying two backs in this manner, the defense is stretched wider, the secondary is locked into certain coverages, and some stunts will make the defense become unsound if they choose to gamble. See Diagram 2–7.

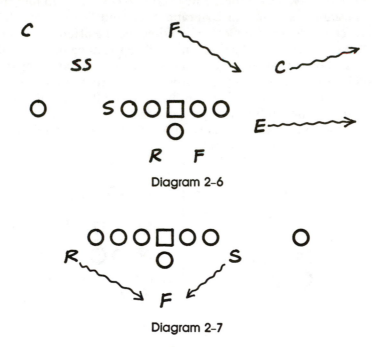

Diagram 2–6

Diagram 2–7

SUMMARY

Each of these tactics is covered in this book as they come into play against the various defenses. You won't use all of these plays on a given Saturday, but you also won't be locked into one method of attack either. There are times when combinations of these ideas may best serve the offense and times when it is to your best advantage to play it straight. Each situation has to be handled separately. You may not choose to attack a particular defense the same way every time. Factors like intelligence, size, and speed vary from player to player, game to game, and year to year. We have presented all the possibilities we know to help find the combination that will best meet your needs in the next game.

These offensive adjustments are not very difficult for the players to learn. When you break all these possibilities down to their components, you find each player learns only a few new things. Most of the learning is on the part of the coach.

Motion

One word can place any player in motion. Each player listens for the one word that affects him.

Fullback—"Fly."

Running Back—"Race."

Slotback—"Scat."

Split End—"Streak."

Tight End—"Jet."

Splitting

To move any player in or out, each player has to listen for only one word.

Split End Tight—"In."

Tight End Out—"Out."

Slotback Flanked—"Wide."

Running Back Winged—"Wing."

Running Back Flanked—"Flank."

Unbalanced

The offense can achieve this in several ways. You can place an end on the opposite side of the line or you can bring a guard over. When you bring the guard over, he is usually aligned outside the tackle to the split side.

Guard Over—"Go."

Tight End Over—"Opposite." (op.)

Split End Over—"See Over."

Formation

What is in a word? Football has a language all its own, so why get locked into another language? We make up our own words that build our own vocabulary, just as the Germans do. When they need a new word, they add together several old words that describe what is wanted. Examples are: Any formation that is strong to the split-end side starts in "S" and formations that are strong to the tight-end (pro-end) side start in "P." Any formation that works out of the I ends with that sound. Any formation that is strong to either side will be denoted in the word: "*S*trong," "*P*ower," "*S*ly," "*P*ly," etc.

The possibilities are endless, and you can make up new formations on the spur of the moment without confusion as long as each player will listen for the word, letter, or phrase that involves him.

3

How to Attack Secondaries with the Belly Option Passing Game

THE BELLY OPTION is primarily a running offense, with a passing game that serves as a supplement. Though option football teams do not live by the pass, that doesn't mean that the pass is not an integral part of the offense.

Running teams generally have a statistically more explosive passing game than teams that live by the pass. The reason is obvious: Since the opponent is geared to stop the run, a well-timed pass can become a game-breaking play. So as you examine the passing game, keep in mind the passing attack's role within the total offensive package.

This chapter examines each type of coverage and then explains the best method for attacking each defender in each type of defense.

ATTACKING MAN COVERAGE

Strengths of Man Coverage

1. Pressure makes it tough on timed patterns.
2. It forces the offense to make adjustment on short and medium routes.
3. Prior to the snap there are no noticeable weak spots.

Weaknesses of Man Coverage

1. There is usually no help for the defender that is beat.
2. It has difficulty handling crossing patterns.
3. It places slower linebackers on faster running backs.

Attacking Strategy

Beating the Onside Cornerback

The Stop pattern is a favorite pass against a man-for-man cornerback. This route evolves from the basic belly option action. The quarterback takes the first three steps of the belly action and comes to balance on the third step just as he completes his fake to the fullback. The split end runs down 6 yards or approximately four steps, then turns back to the quarterback to receive the quick pass. The ball should be in the air as the receiver makes his plant to come back to the football. This pattern is shown in Diagram 3–1. The success of this play depends on the split end's ability to drive the corner off prior to making the break back to the line of scrimmage.

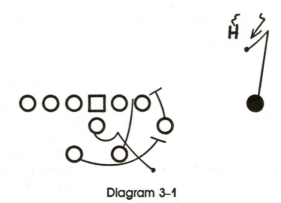

Diagram 3–1

Beating the Strong Safety

The strong safety will usually be responsible for the slotback in man coverage. If the slotback blocks, the strong safety will fill at the corner, taking the pitch or quarterback on the option unless he is involved in a stunt. If the slot releases off the line, he usually covers him for the pass.

There are two slotback patterns that threaten the responsibility of the strong safety. First is the basic arc pass. From this route the offense still has the potential to run the option. See Diagram 3–2. On the snap, the slotback takes three steps to the outside as though he is trying to gain outside leverage on the defensive end. After the third step, he turns straight upfield and looks for the ball over his inside shoulder. This places the strong safety in a difficult predicament. If he comes up to aid the forcing unit on the option, the slotback will be wide open for the pass in the seam area. If he stays back to cover the slotback, the quarterback will have the option not to throw the ball but keep it or pitch to the running back.

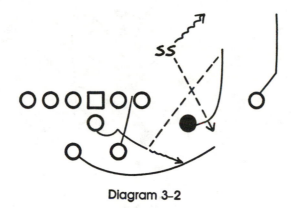

Diagram 3–2

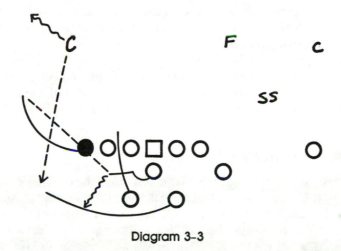

Diagram 3–3

This is the basic play of the triple option and theoretically cannot be stopped by a seven-front defense or an eight-front that uses the strong safety to cover the slotback. We do not advocate this pass versus a team that covers the slotback with the free safety. In that situation, we prefer to run the arc pass to the tight-end side, since they are now playing a monster defense. See Diagram 3–3.

The other pass is a potential touchdown play every time it is completed against man coverage. This is the quick-up route to the slotback.

On the snap, the slotback releases into the flat, aims for a depth of about 10 yards, and looks for the ball over his outside shoulder. The quarterback ride fakes the fullback, comes to balance on the fifth step, and pump fakes the split end on the curl. Without hesitation, he resets and arcs a pass to the slotback as he turns up the sideline, looking over his inside shoulder. It is important that the quarterback does not delay between the

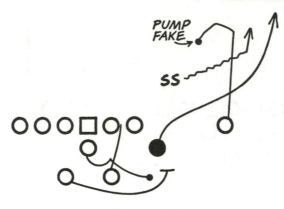

Diagram 3-4

curl fake and the pass to the slotback on the up route. If he delays, the free safety or the cornerback will recover and get under the ball. The total distance of the throw should not be more than 18 to 20 yards downfield. See Diagram 3-4. The slotback must be sure to get width before he turns upfield. Too often the slotback becomes so anxious to get open that he turns upfield prematurely and places himself in the path of the cornerback covering the curl man or the free safety pursuing across the field.

Beating the Free Safety

The free safety is the player who usually stops the option because he is coming from the backside and often does not get picked up in the blocking scheme. His angle of pursuit gives him excellent vision of the option as it develops, which encourages him to "let it all hang out" as he closes on the option area. When this situation is present, the best play in your attack is the post pattern to the split end.

The quarterback should make a good play fake on the outside belly or wide veer to the fullback, then retreat a total of seven steps from the point of the snap and set up for the throw. This should give the free safety enough time to commit on the run action. The split end will charge off the line, pushing the strong corner deep prior to making the post move at six yards. This action is the same as the release he used on the regular belly-option play. This gives the free safety a read similar to the one he gets on the running play. After an outside head fake, the split will break hard for the post, looking for the ball over his inside shoulder. He must *not* continue across the field into the area being defended by the weakside corner. If he finds that he is getting too far beyond the midline, he must turn upfield toward the goalpost. As shown in Diagram 3-5, the slotback blocks the onside end instead of releasing upfield. This aids in occupying the free and strong safeties in run support.

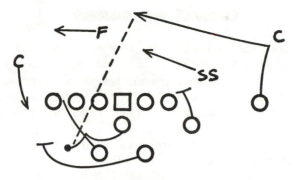

Diagram 3-5

Beating the Offside Cornerback

If the free safety is centerfield conscious and the strong safety is the player given the primary run support role, the tight-end drag becomes a very big play. In an effort to occupy the free safety, the slotback must release quickly and run directly at the free safety, forcing him to honor this action. We know that the strong safety has a difficult double read, as he is responsible for the streaking slotback and at the same time must take the pitch back on the slow developing option play. This same strong safety is the quarterback's read after the third step. If the strong safety drops into the secondary, the quarterback must continue to threaten the corner as he rolls behind the lead block of his running back. There should be no one to pick up the slotback if he clears the defensive end, unless the strong safety honors his threat. The tight end should break off the line just as he does on the option, but as he crosses the field, he should locate the streaking slotback and slide closely underneath him. When he crosses under the slotback he should aim for a spot about 18 yards deep, midway between the slotback and the split end, who is also streaking down the sideline. See Diagram 3-6.

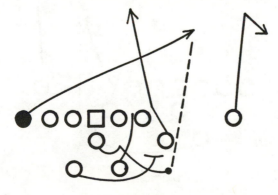

Diagram 3-6

BEATING THE LINEBACKERS

In most cases, the linebackers are responsible for any fake into the line by the running back or fullback. If they do not tackle these backs on their fake, then you will be getting your fastest receivers on the slowest defenders. It is not as easy to complete this pass because of time needed to get these receivers into the open field. There is no special pattern used by these two backs to get open.

The key is for the three primary receivers to clear both the safety and the two cornerbacks deep or across the field, away from the spot you designate for the setbacks to run. Diagram 3–7 shows one of the most popular passes used in defeating man-for-man coverage by the linebackers. The slotback runs the same clear-out route he uses on the tight-end drag, and the split end runs a 14-yard sideline route to occupy the onside corner-back. The fullback will run an outside–veer fake outside the onside tackle. If he clears the wash at the line of scrimmage, then he should press quickly straight up the field in that seam, looking for the ball over his outside shoulder.

This pass can be released as soon as he gets leverage on the linebacker, so he can look early. His aiming point should be the area mid-way between the slotback and the split end at a spot about 18 yards deep. The quarterbacks' steps are the same as on the tight-end drag pass. The quarterback should set up to throw both of these passes, unless he shows a very special proficiency to pass on the run. During the heat of combat most quarterbacks will give the receiver too much lead when they throw on the move.

Another very successful variation of this pass is to fake the fullback on the cutback trap and have him slide out to the backside and be picked up by

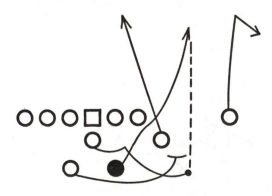

Diagram 3–7

the backside linebacker. Most teams will designate the frontside linebacker to pick up the first fake into the line and the far linebacker to pick up the second fake. Frequently, the backside linebacker will let the fullback slide by him as he flows to the onside hook area. The tight end will clear across the field, just as he does on the drag pass. Often the fullback will pop out of the backside of the defense and be wide open at about 12 yards. The quarterback should set up on the seventh step and throw the ball over the fullback's backside shoulder as he runs toward the far flag.

These passes may seem easy to defend by giving the linebackers definite dive responsibilities, but after you become aware of the complications they encounter on certain running situations, you should return to this section and reread the segment on play-action passing. When both the run and pass aspects of the belly-option attack are blended together, the problems encountered by the linebackers are far more complex.

ATTACKING ZONE COVERAGE

Strengths of Zone Coverage

1. Each defender can always get help from other defenders.
2. A weak defender can play it safe and work deep behind the receiver.
3. It is easier to handle flood patterns and unusual formations.

Weakness of Zone Coverage

1. It can be attacked in the seams between the zones.
2. It is difficult to put pressure on the passer and still be sound in the undercoverage.

Attacking Strategy

Beating the Strongside Corner

The most consistent method of attacking the strong corner is the sideline or out pattern. Since that defender usually is responsible for the deep third of the field, he will give ground to protect against the deep threat. The strong safety will be slow getting underneath the sideline threat because he will be temporarily obligated to contain the option play. The 15-yard break is the most effective depth for the sideline route. If the cut comes too soon, the defender will not be pushed off enough to open a seam in the coverage. If the route is much deeper, the ball will be in the air too long and the corner can react in time to make the play. See Diagram 3–8.

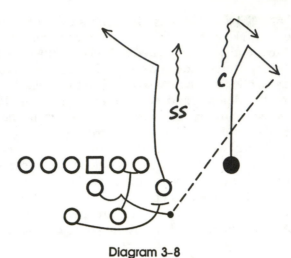

Diagram 3-8

The quarterback should set up to throw this pass on his fifth step. To further aid in the isolation of the strong corner, the slotback will run a post route to hold the free safety and linebacker.

Beating the Strong Safety

A route that is complementary to the sideline is the split-end curl. Both patterns should look exactly alike until the final break. The curl is designed to threaten the area covered by that strong safety while he is honoring his run commitment. If the split end aligns too tight, the strong corner can get help from the free safety or onside linebacker. It is important for him to align at least 17 yards from the tackle when the ball is snapped. The slotback is integral to the success of this pattern since the defense usually keys him for run or pass. When this happens it is best to keep him in to block the defensive end. If the strong safety reads the slotback and widens with him as he breaks on the out pattern, then it is better to use the slot to clear this defender from under the curl zone, as shown in Diagram 3-9.

When the zone is secondary or particularly loose, then it is most advisable to take immediate advantage of this situation with the two-step slant pass. On the slant the quarterback takes the first two steps of the belly series action and the split end will slant behind the strong safety. This pass looks easy to complete on paper, but it can be very difficult if the quarterback and split end don't have it timed properly. The secret to a successful slant is for the quarterback not to look for the end slanting in, but to read the strong safety and onside linebacker. He should pass the ball directly between these two defenders so neither one is in position to deflect the

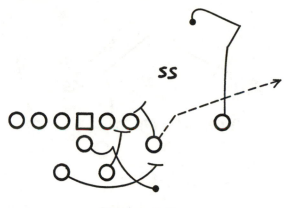

Diagram 3–9

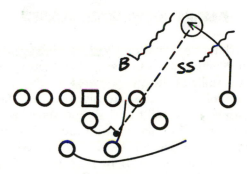

Diagram 3–10

pass. The split end should aim his route to get midway between these two defenders; when the pattern is timed in this manner, the percentage of completion will jump considerably and the interception ratio will go way down. See Diagram 3-10.

When the defenses uses the strong safety to offer backside support on weakside option plays, the slotback-post pass is a very big play. In the belly scheme, the weak side is attacked only when the defense overcompensates to the strong side. When they overcompensate, the free safety has a long way to go to support the pitch to the weakside. Because both safeties are overextended, they must strain to get back into position to cover the deep third and the deep middle. This causes the post to the slotback to become a potential touchdown pass. The quarterback should set up on the sixth step if he is rolling left. He will hit the slotback just after he breaks for the goalpost following the inside release on the defensive end as shown in Diagram 3-11.

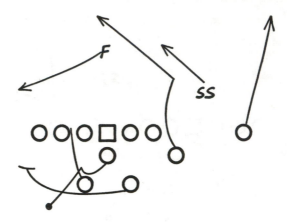

Diagram 3-11

BEATING THE WEAKSIDE CORNER

To attack this defender consistently, the bootleg pass is the most effective play. The option action starts to the split end (strong side), and after a deliberate ride to the fullback the quarterback will plant and roll back to the tight-end side. As he rolls across the offensive backfield, he will increase his depth to about 9 yards. The tight end should start his route exactly the same as he does on the option play, but on the sixth step he should plant and sprint back toward the flag on the side he started. This action forces the weakside cornerback to retreat or be beat deep. The slotback releases inside, crosses the face of the defense, and should achieve a depth of about 8 yards as he comes out the far side of the defense. The quarterback's first read is to the weak corner. If the corner honors the tight end, the slotback should be open short. If someone in the undercoverage picks up the slotback, there probably won't be any containment pressure on the quarterback to prevent him from turning upfield and running the ball.

On the bootleg pass the offensive line must alter the blocking scheme to protect a passing area that will develop opposite the normal throwing zone. To achieve this, the protectors on the tight-end side (tackle, guard, and center) will cup protect with their backs to the tight-end side instead of the other way. The splitside tackle and fullback will block solid to the split side and the running back will wall off the defensive end. The pulling guard will become the quarterback's personal protector. He will pull flat toward the tight-end side of two steps, then belly away from the line on a 45-degree angle until he is in position to seal in the end. If the defensive end removes himself from the pursuit, then the puller should continue to flow out and up the field, anticipating a quarterback run. The quarterback fake to the fullback is critical to beating the weakside contain man. If the quarterback stays with the fullback long enough to get a full-arm ride, the

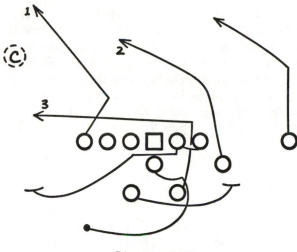

Diagram 3-12

backside defensive end will usually adjust his charge to maintain a good pursuit angle on the fullback. When the quarterback disengages from the fullback, he must place the ball in his left hip watchpocket with both hands. It is important that he does not attempt to use a one-handed bootleg maneuver. This usually leaves the ball hanging out in plain view of everyone on the backside. If he can successfully hide the ball for the next two steps, the defensive end will have lost his leverage to the pulling guard. Since the defender and the quarterback are going in opposite directions, there are times when it is not necessary to block him. See Diagram 3-12.

BEATING THE LINEBACKERS

To defeat the linebackers you must exert a constant vertical stretch on the defense. To do this, the slotback will release as though he is going to run a clearing pattern on the free safety. At a depth of 12 yards he will blend into the area between the inside linebackers, settling midway between these two players. If the ball is not in the air when he reaches that point, he should work directly toward the passer. From the time he clears the line, he is the hot receiver and must keep constant eye contact with the inside linebackers. If he recognizes a blitz developing, he must cut the pattern short to provide the quarterback with an outlet man. If there is no blitz, he will run the full route. The fullback also plays a key role in helping handle the blitz. When it develops, he is responsible for picking up the blitz linebacker. If it doesn't develop, he becomes the outlet receiver just across the line of scrimmage. His job is to visually locate the open spot between the linebackers when he fakes in the line. When he has located the open area, he then stops there and turns to face the passer. The quarterback sets up on the fifth step and reads the frontside inside linebacker. If this defender commits to the slotback and takes away the pass over the middle, he should dump the ball to the waiting fullback. The fullback has to be sure that he is not moving when he makes the catch. He must catch the ball, turn, find the linebackers, and run straight upfield between them. The safety valve must be aware that this is not supposed to be a big play reception, but one that will permit us to maintain ball control. Even so, we have averaged close to 20 yards per reception with this pass to the fullback. See Diagram 3–13.

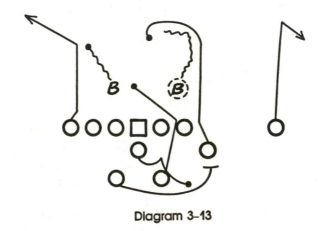

Diagram 3–13

ATTACKING COMBINATION COVERAGES

There are some very complex pass coverages now filtering down from the professional level. These combinations of man and zone defense are designed to thwart the complex professional passing attacks, but are not always the easiest things to implement at either the college or the high school levels. Nevertheless, let's add these defensive secondary schemes to our examination of defensive strategies.

Attacking Strategies

There are teams that desire to play a man-for-man coverage underneath and a zone coverage deep, but they should never be doing it after the first period against an option football team. If any option team releases the primary receivers and runs a triple-option attack against a team playing a combination coverage, it will be left with no one to take the pitch on the option play. Though this type of coverage is great against dropback passing teams, it would not be sound against a team that runs an option offense. Thus we will focus our examination of combo coverages to man on one side and zone on the other. The favorite combination coverage is man to the strong side and zone to the weak. With this approach the defense feels they can always get an extra defender into run support by bringing him from the backside; if they meet action to the side of zone protection, they will remain sound.

The offensive strategy in this situation is quite simple. If they are weakest in the area where they are playing man coverage, then the offensive strategist should revert to those patterns that are most effective to the front side against man defenses, as shown earlier in this chapter. If you feel the area being protected by zone coverage is the weakest, then use those pass plays that are best against the side that is zone.

An example of how to beat the weakest deep defender is shown in Diagram 3–4 and on the sideline in Diagram 3–6. Both are very good calls. To beat the man theory deep, run the fullback flood as shown in Diagram 3–7. In the short areas, the slant shown in Diagram 3–10 or the arc in Diagram 3–2 are examples of methods to beat the short zone by getting into the seams.

This philosophy is not an escape from taking an honest look at combination coverages, but is a realistic way of breaking these schemes down to their simplest components and attacking them as they really are: a man or zone defense at the point of attack. Too often coaches make the game more complex than it is by over intellectualizing it. If you keep it simple, it is easier for both you and your players to understand what is trying to be accomplished.

4

How to Attack the Four-Three Battery with the Belly T Running Game

BEFORE SUCCESSFULLY ATTACKING any defense, you must be aware of the strengths and weaknesses inherent in each defensive scheme. Therefore, the strengths and weaknesses of each defensive battery will be listed with regard to their effect on the belly option attack.

Strengths of the Four-Three Defense

1. With three linebackers, the defense will have good pursuit in run support. (See Diagram 4–1.)
2. By covering the guards, it becomes difficult to block the middle linebacker.
3. It is a good defense for stunting, especially the inside four-three alignment.
4. It is a good defense for stunting at the perimeter.

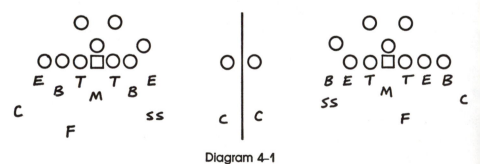

Diagram 4–1

Weaknesses of the Four-Three Defense

1. It is an easy defense to trap, especially if the outside linebackers are aligned wide, as in the pro-forty.
2. It is weak against inside counters in the pro alignment when the middle linebacker overpursues.
3. More quality athletes are needed for this defense to be successful. It requires three people capable of playing both run and pass at the key linebacker positions.
4. The middle bubble is weak against a straight-ahead ball control attack.

Attacking Strategy

1. Run directly at this defense with man- or trap-blocking.
2. Run counter plays behind the flowing middle linebacker.
3. Isolate the middle linebacker so he can be angle blocked.
4. Run option plays at the perimeter to pressure the players with dual run and pass responsibilities.

Running Outside

The theory of belly option football is to slow the pursuit of the middle linebacker with the attack's complete running package (fullback dive, option, and the inside counter). Assuming the belly option can achieve this goal, you can proceed with your first objective. You must read the free safety and attack according to his alignment. (See Diagrams 4–2a, 4–2b, and 4–2c.) If the free safety aligns in position "A," he cannot be effective in stopping the option to the split end. Likewise, if he is aligned in position "C," he will not be effective in stopping the option series to the tight end. If the defense chooses to play their secondary balanced, you should attack to the strong side. If the defense wants to monster up to the strong side (split end), you should run to the tight end (or weak side). Either of the above

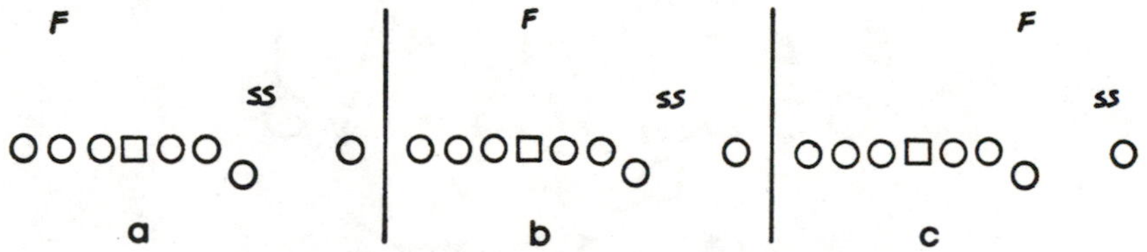

Diagram 4–2

schemes should force the free safety into position "B," which is the toughest alignment for him to play. In the middle he must not only offer support to either side but also become the keystone of the pass coverage (refer to Chapter 3). Once the location of the free safety is established, attention is directed to the strong safety. He is now vulnerable to the run or pass potentials of the option attack.

By running the option series at the strong safety with arc-blocking (see Diagram 4–3), he is placed in a position of conflict. Should he defend the run or pass? In this instance he needs the support of the free safety, who must also honor his own obligations to the deep middle zone.

Also, the strong safety can be easily influenced into quick-run support. By having the slotback down block, he is given a definite run read. He may have a tendency to attack the pitch lane too quickly in an effort to make up the ground he yielded on his initial alignment. As he flows to gain leverage on the pitch out, he becomes susceptible to the outside veer attack of the fullback (see Diagram 4–4).

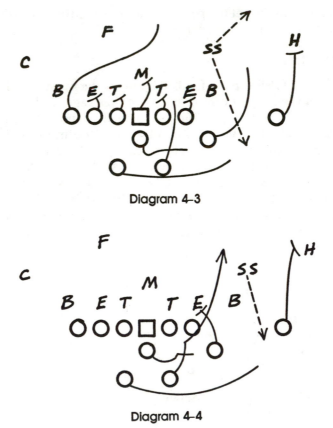

Diagram 4–3

Diagram 4–4

So far in this chapter we have covered the outside attack on the assumption that the offense would be able to deal effectively with the middle linebacker. But there are times that this cannot be achieved, so you are forced to make adjustments to prevent him from bringing the offense to a grinding halt.

At Coatesville, the first step in trying to neutralize this player would be to go unbalanced. At this point, many coaches turn off, because they think going unbalanced will be too complicated and will create a difficult learning problem for their players. They argue that going unbalanced may create just as much confusion for the offense as for the defense and neutralize any advantage gained by going unbalanced. It is our experience that no confusion develops if only one player makes the adjustment to create the unbalanced situation. Only this player gets a new blocking rule and the rule is kept very simple. The rule states: On all inside plays block inside linebacker, and on outside plays block inside on or off the LOS. Assuming you can teach one player to make this adjustment, you can effectively go unbalanced.

The defense must make a decision: either move down or be outflanked at the perimeter. Generally, the defense will adjust in one of three ways (Diagrams 4–5a, 4–5b, and 4–5c). They can slide the whole defense half a man to the strong side as shown in Diagram 4–5a (the most popular move); or they can slide their linebackers a full man to the strength, creat-

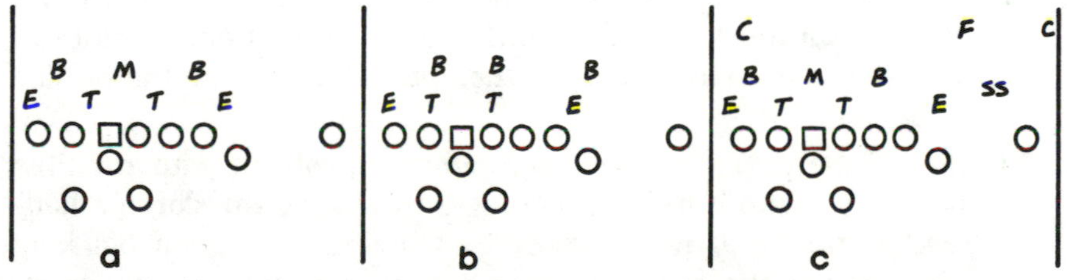

Diagram 4-5

ing a new defensive look as in Diagram 4–5b; or they can keep their forcing unit in place and rotate their secondary. This adjustment would bring us back to the original proposition. But in each of these adjustments the middle linebacker becomes vulnerable to the down block. When this happens, all the pressure is placed on the outside linebacker or end (whichever one aligns on the slotback). The only way the four-three defense can reestablish its principles would be to move down a full man. This would regain the end man in the forcing units leverage and permit the middle linebacker to flow more freely behind covered offensive blockers. But the obvious problem arises: How will the defense be able to handle the option that hits the corner so quickly to the short side? (See Diagram 4–6.)

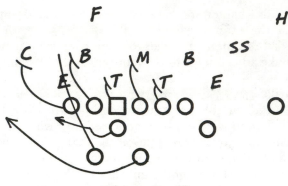

Diagram 4-6

Variations to Aid the Outside Running Game

1. If you choose not to go unbalanced on the option but are having trouble with a strong middle linebacker, the strongside tackle and the fullback can switch responsibilities on the arc option (see Diagram 4-7). The tackle will seal off the middle linebacker (MLB) and the fullback becomes responsible for the number 2 LB after his strong belly ride fake. But, if the ride is weak, the outside backer will be able to bounce outside and support the option.

2. If number 3 tries to cross the tight end or slotback's face in an effort to put quick pressure on the ride, the tight end or slot can block this man in and place all the option burdens on the middle linebacker.

3. Also, if the defensive end is creating a problem with multiple charges, you can simplify his charges by placing the slot in a half-back position, creating a power I set. Using his regular blocking rules, the slot attacks the number 3 man from this location, creating a loaded-option read. If the defender crashes hard to abort the fullback ride, he can be easily sealed to the inside by the slotback. As the outside linebacker recognizes the load block, his normal reaction is to challenge the slotback. This creates a large running lane for the outside veer (see Diagram 4-8).

4. In conjunction with the loaded veer, the load fake Arc Option provides a solid complimentary play (see Diagram 4-9). The outside linebacker recognizes the load block and attacks the slotback, who passes him up as he proceeds toward his block on the strong safety. This blocking scheme creates considerable havoc with teams that like to use multiple charges at the corner. Instead of the offense reacting to the defensive charges, the defenses end up adjusting to the offensive schemes.

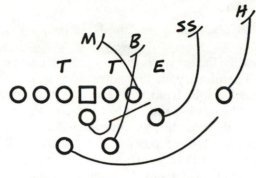

Diagram 4-7

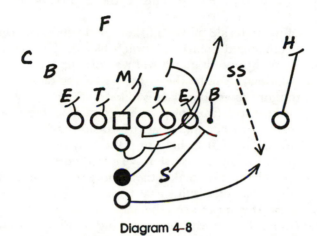

Diagram 4-8

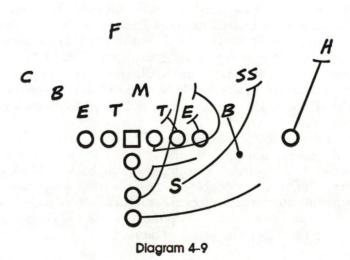

Diagram 4-9

Running Inside

The most popular philosophy used in attacking the four-three defense suggests running directly at it with base (or man-for-man) blocking.
Obviously, the middle linebacker is the key player to be beaten if the dive is
to be successful. Therefore, your first adjustment would be for the splitside
guard to increase his split from the center to three feet. Normally the
defense will adjust by moving the tackle down into the gap. If he aligns on
the split guard's inside shoulder, the fullback will try to hit the line as close
to the guard's outside foot as possible. The center will fire out for the
middle linebacker, who will be shuffling toward the dive hole. The center
cannot block him back away from the hole, but because of the wide split,
the center has more operating room to run the MLB past the hole, permitting the fullback to hit the dive tight to the guard, behind the flowing
linebacker.

If the defensive tackle moves all the way down to the center's shoulder, then the center and guard will switch blocks. The center will scoop
block the tackle and the split guard will wall off the linebacker. This time
the fullback's landmark will be the inside leg of the tackle. This provides
the center with more room to make his block on the gap tackle. In contrast
to the college four-three (as shown in Diagram 4-1), the straight dive or
speed is very effective when aimed at the outside linebacker (OLB). This
forces the MLB to flow fast to help stop the play or the defensive tackle
(DT) must definitely align on the offensive guard's outside shoulder to take
away the bubble. The former makes the middle bubble vulnerable with no
linebacker while the latter is still suspect with the MLB forced to cover a
large middle area. If you can keep the MLB at home, then the cross block
between the G and T is an effective attacking weapon against the college
four-three.

If the tackle will not adjust down on the split, the dive is aimed directly
at your guard, and the fullback must cut off the guard's block. Normal flow
will carry the middle linebacker and defensive tackle to the outside, so the
dive usually breaks over the center-guard gap. If the offside defensive
tackle pinches down to stop the inside dive or "speed" play that ends up
hitting over the center, you can fold block the center and offside guard to
cut off the offside tackle with the center and let the folding-off guard take
the flowing middle linebacker.

When facing the pro four-three with the outside linebacker in the
number 3 location, trap-blocking the dive has been very successful (see
Diagram 4-10). The dive rule requires the slotback to block the inside
linebacker. This creates a double-team on the most dangerous defender.
As long as the quarterback gives the fullback a good ride, the outside
linebacker will not be a threat to stop the dive. He will position himself to
stop the keep or pitch phase of the option.

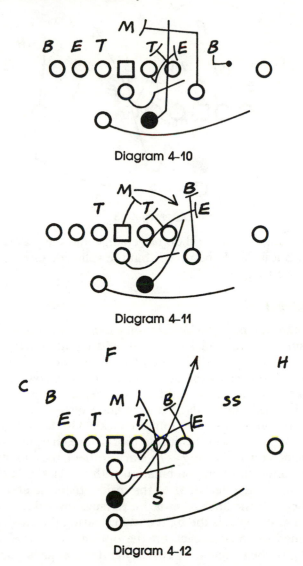

Diagram 4-10

Diagram 4-11

Diagram 4-12

By examining Diagram 4–11 you can see that the same blocking scheme is not as effective against the college four-three. The slotback must block the number 2 linebacker requiring the center to single block the middle linebacker. Because of the center's poor leverage, you cannot block this defense successfully with rule-blocking unless you go unbalanced.

When aligning unbalanced with the slot in the power I location, the dive is once more an effective play, if the defense does not adjust its front down to the unbalanced (see Diagram 4–12). The best part of this offensive adjustment is that no blocking changes are needed. If the defense does

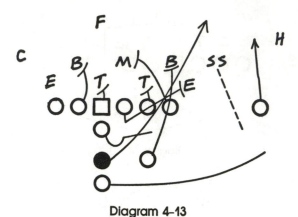

Diagram 4-13

adjust a full man, the rules still do not change and the play can still be run successfully. But it should be noted that the split-side tackle has a tougher assignment (see Diagram 4–13).

Off Tackle

When the defensive tackle becomes dive conscious and moves to a headup position on your tackle, you should try to run the outside dive instead of the inside speed dive. The offensive tackle can then single block his man inside, thus freeing the tight end or slot to go down to the inside on the linebacker. If the tackle is aligned wide, he must be combination blocked by the tackle and end. The tight end's technique on the combination block is to align at five feet from the tackle. On the snap of the ball, he must take a lateral step with his inside foot before charging upfield. If the defensive tackle's hip is showing as he starts upfield, the end must executive an aggressive angle block in combination with the tackle. If the tackle has successfully turned the defender to the inside, then the end will continue upfield and cut off the linebacker as he pursues toward the running lane. The inside lateral step aids the tight end in clearing the outside linebacker, who is assigned the quarterback on the option. Of course, this blocking method will give the secondary a run key and cause quick pursuit, keeping the gains to a minimum.

When the fast-filling secondary support becomes a problem, an arc release by the tight end will help if the tackle is able to single-block the defender on his nose. The arc release gives the defense a pass read and will not be as inclined to fill quickly on the outside veer. The most important factors in making this play successful are the ride of the quarterback and the course of the fullback. The fullback must aim at the inside leg of the offensive tackle for the first three steps. If he does not convince the defense that you are running the inside dive, normal pursuit angles will cause all the offensive linemen to lose their blocking angles, making the play ineffec-

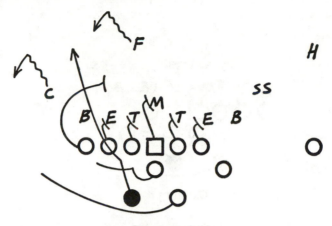

Diagram 4–14

tive. The quarterback must also give his most convincing ride to permit the blockers to gain the much needed leverage for their blocks.

In short yardage situations when a few key yards are necessary, you can run the outside veer with an arc block to the middle linebacker (see Diagram 4–14). This temporarily gives the defense a pass read, while permitting the end/slot to wall off the fast flowing inside linebacker. At Widener, we have found the following Dream play variations to be helpful against the four-three.

Countering

One of the most effective counter plays against the four-three is the quick slant dive (described earlier in the chapter). But, when it is run as a counter, it will be trap-blocked or folded from the backside (see Diagrams 4–15 and 4–16). By folding the backside guard around to the middle

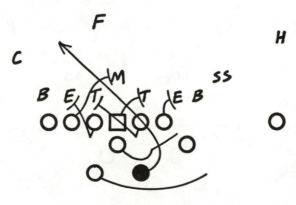

Diagram 4–15

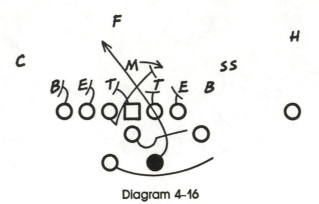

Diagram 4-16

linebacker, every blocker has an angle, and the fast-flowing middle linebacker has lost his leverage on the ballcarrier. If the defensive guards are superior football players, the slant dive should be trap-blocked with a false pull to influence the far side guard.

There are two delay counters used against the four-three. Both are always among our best game-breaking plays. Versus the pro type four-three, we at Coatesville like the tailback handback trap. Against the pro defense, the middle linebacker has dive responsibility. Consequently, he cannot help on any counteraction. This places the burden of stopping slow-developing plays on the far linebacker. From the wide alignment, he can be walled off because he is two players removed from the point of attack (see Diagram 4-17). *Note:* If the backside defensive guard does a superior job of keeping the offensive guard from releasing on the middle linebacker, the trap should be moved one hole wider. The offensive tackle will close down

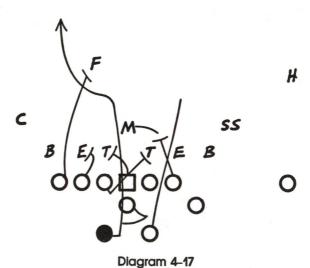

Diagram 4-17

on the pinching guard and the trap will be executed on the tackle. Be careful to advise the back that the hole will open one man wider.

When facing the college four-three with the outside linebackers inside the ends, the wingback scissors play is the most effective delay counter. By aligning over the tackle, this linebacker is more effective against the tailback counter, making it necessary to run counters wider (see Diagram 4–18). The scissors can be blocked several ways. The most popular has been to show pass the backside, letting the tackle and end rush, thus exposing the corner and outside linebacker to angle-block from the tight end and split guard. If the guard to the side of the counter has trouble handling the defensive lineman on his nose, the play can be fold-blocked in the same manner as the slant trap. The major difference between the two blocking schemes is the route the slotback takes after the hand-off. If the play is pass-blocked, the running lane develops toward the flag. But when fold-blocked, the running lane is open toward the goalposts (see Diagram 4–19). We prefer to pass-block this play so it will break all the way back against the grain. When we are forced to run it north and south, the average gain is less because the defense has better pursuit angles. On the other hand, we have experienced success when the play hits north and south.

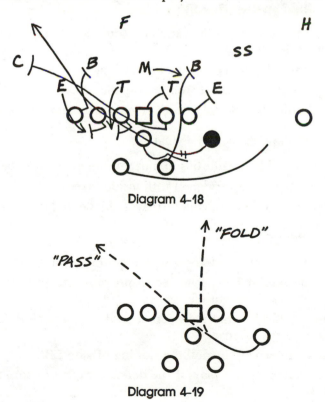

Diagram 4–18

Diagram 4–19

5

How to Attack
the Fifty-Two Battery
with the Running Game

THE BELLY OFFENSE was designed specifically to beat the basic fifty-two. Over the years the fifty-two has been altered and presents more problems than the original fifty-two, but it can certainly be attacked successfully.

Strengths of the Fifty-Two Defense

1. It is strong outside when the end (number 3) aligns outside the tight end/slotback.
2. The inside linebackers provide excellent run support.
3. Alignment allows great stunting capabilities.
4. Total utilization of defense gives good pass-and-run balance.

Weaknesses of the Fifty-Two Defense

1. "Bubbles" (LBs off line of scrimmage) over guards can be attacked.
2. Option plays are very good with inside fakes.
3. Flowing LBs allow for counterplays to hit behind their movement.

Attacking Strategy

1. Run directly at this defense with man- or trap-blocking.
2. Run outside at the perimeter to pressure the players with dual run-and-pass responsibilities.
3. Run off tackle when you can seal off the inside defenders by adjusting the offense.
4. Run counterplays behind the flowing offside LB.
5. Run counteroption plays if the defense adjusts to stop the inside plays.

Running Outside

The option play with the onside guard leading is always our first choice for a big outside running play, as is shown in Diagram 5–1. It's better to run it with rule-blocking whenever possible by having the onside tackle and slotback block down on the two defenders to their inside, and the onside guard pulling to lead the pitch on the running track. When the onside seal by your onside tackle and slotback can be accomplished, your quarterback is placed in a one-on-one battle with the defensive end. Most of the time the end is given quarterback responsibility, permitting you to utilize the desired pitch out to the trailing back. The pitch back will get on the track behind the pulling guard, who is responsible for the remaining defender available to stop the play. By staying on the running track, the pitch back will set up the pulling guard's block and make a big gain by cutting off this blocker's helmet.

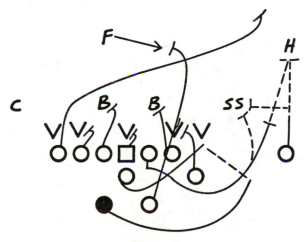

Diagram 5–1

The key for a constantly successful option play is to properly control the technique employed by the onside defensive tackle. Problems develop when that defender does a good job of keeping your tackle from releasing to the inside linebacker. In this instance you want the slotback and tackle to switch assignments, having the slot go down on the linebacker and the tackle reach-block on the defender assigned to tie him up. You will also apply this technique to a tackle that is using a pinching technique. Often there is doubt before the snap as to the exact intentions of this defender, so you must teach your slotback and tackle a combination technique to handle properly the uncertainty of the situation. When the combination block is employed, your tackle will step for the defensive tackle's outside hip and aim to get his head to the outside of the defender, while the slotback or tight end will align five feet outside the tackle and execute the same technique he uses on the outside veer off-tackle play.

If the defensive end is doing a superior job of keeping the slot or tight end from releasing to the inside, you will have to make a further adjustment. The tackle will fold-block to the linebacker and the tight end or slotback will block down on the defender to their inside, as shown in Diagram 5-2. This technique is more suited to the tight-end side than the slot side, because the slot usually has enough room to clear the line due to his recessed position prior to the snap, while the tackle must pull deeper to clear the slotback, delaying him from reaching the linebacker.

The second approach to this play is to arc-block, as shown in Diagram 5-3. This plan is used when the defensive back responsible for contain reads the guard pull scheme and gets up too fast to be blocked in the conventional manner. In this case, you can employ man-for-man blocking

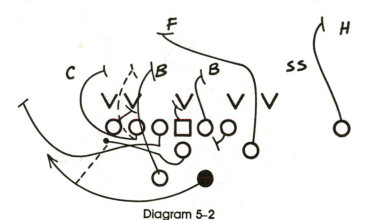

Diagram 5-2

Diagram 5-3

along most of the front and arc release the onside slotback or tight end. The arc release of the slotback should keep the containing defensive back off the line while he attempts to determine run or pass. The time it takes for this defender to make his decision helps the slotback gain the needed advantage for his block.

The rest of the play remains basically the same, except for a few technique variations necessary to handle a stunt from the potentially dangerous onside tackle. The onside guard and tackle will scoop or reach step toward their count man in an effort to pick up any potential inside slant by the defensive tackle. If that defender is angling to the inside, the guard will pick him up on the second step and the tackle will continue through for the scraping frontside linebacker. If there is no stunt, these two blockers will try to get the head to the outside hip of their count block on the second step. These two blocks should be aided by the belly fake inside the defensive tackle.

Another variation that offers a combination of both rule and arc-man blocking can be very effective when you see some combination of these various defensive tactics. But, it should be noted that this scheme is dependent once again on the onside tackle's ability to control the defensive tackle. This alternative blocking is referred to as rule-arc-around. See Diagram 5-4. The onside tackle blocks the defensive tackle as mentioned and the slotback arc releases to hold the strong safety, but folds around the end and back to the inside linebacker. The guard pulls as in the basic option play and should have a better chance of success, since the strong safety has been held momentarily by the slotback's arc release. Both the pulling guard and slotback must be prepared to turn up abruptly if either the strong safety or linebacker stunt inside the defensive end, which would happen when the

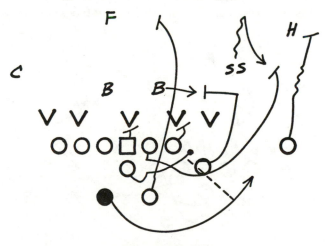

Diagram 5-4

defensive end is assigned pitch responsibility. If these blockers can pick up the stunt in question, the option will usually break for a large gain. Naturally, the quarterback would end up keeping the ball versus this defensive ploy.

In the last chapter we talked of the importance of controlling the man over the center. The same principle holds true in the fifty-two defense. We have assumed up to this point that the center would be able to neutralize the middle guard. But the basic theory of the fifty-two defense is built upon the idea that the middle guard should not be single-blocked by the center. When we face a team that has a superior athlete playing this position, alternative blocking schemes must be used. By using the unbalanced scheme the defense is forced to make the same decisions that were required of the four-three defense. They can move the whole defensive front a full man, adjust a half man, or keep the front solid and fully rotate the secondary to the unbalanced side if they don't want to be outflanked.

Though the blocking scheme varies, the overall philosophy used to attack a seven-front defense remains the same. If they adjust the front a full man to the long side, you will have achieved your goal of getting an angle-block on this outstanding defender and be able to neutralize his special contribution to the success of this defensive scheme. If they only adjust a half man, you may need to use the slotback set in the backfield as a helper on him. Diagram 5–5 shows how you would attempt to seal off his pursuit and at the same time not jeopardize any of the other players' assignments. The slotback may be cheated up if necessary without giving away the play. From here he will be in position to help on several other running or passing plays.

If the defense doesn't move at all, the nose guard would still be in a strong position on the center, but everyone else on the defense would be outflanked. The blocking can be changed to arc-blocking and any of sev-

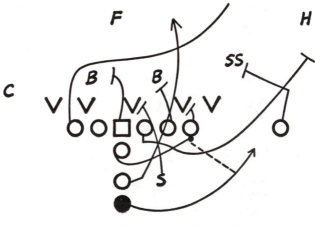

Diagram 5–5

eral players can be used to help on this defender. The single best adjustment we have found is to move the unbalanced guard to the other side of
the center and give him sole responsibility for the nose guard. While the
defense gets a completely different offensive read, no other player needs a
rule change. See Diagram 5–6.

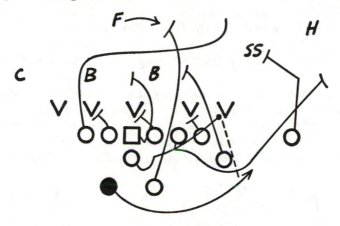

Diagram 5–6

Though we draw up every play going for a touchdown, in reality it
seldom happens the way it is drawn. So before moving on to the other
attack areas of the fifty defense, let's examine the spots that break down
most often. After years of charting tackles from the fifty defense, we have
found that the offside linebacker and the free safety make most of the
tackles on the option play. Therefore, extra effort must be put into neu-
tralizing these two people. In the first several years we ran the belly option,
we had the offside guard show pass for two counts before he moved out.
This gave the linebacker a full-flow pass read; he would take deep pursuit,
look for pass, or turn back on the dragging tight end. But as time passed
this key did not always give us the results we sought. Now we fold the guard
immediately and try to get in the linebacker's face quickly. This, in conjunction with the scissors threat, should neutralize him enough for the
pitchback to make the corner. Also, the offside guard should be the first
one to tell us when it is time to run the scissors. When the linebacker is
flowing too fast for our guard to get in his face, he should alert the coaches.
The counter is given top priority in the game plan.

We place two players in the free safety's path, because he has always
been the number one tackler when we run the option. If our fullback is not
tackled on his dive fake, he is to continue downfield and try to get between
the free safety and the running lane. When he makes this block, the option
usually goes all the way. The other player we tentatively assign to block the
free safety is the tight end or offside slotback. This player can get on the
track in front of the pitchback if he hustles and takes the proper course to
the running lane. He is taught to clear the linebacker depth, then sprint

directly across the field on a course parallel to the line of scrimmage. Once he gets to the running lane he is to stay on it and look for the free safety or off corner pursuing further upfield.

There are times when the free safety can be frozen in centerfield by the post-pass threat of the tight end. When this condition is present, we will split the tight end 8 yards from the tackle and run him on the post route each time we call the option. If the free safety and offside corner will honor his pass threat into their deep zone, the fullback will have plenty of time to get on the running track in front of the pitchback, following his fake into the line.

We have also found the counteroption an excellent antidote for the fast-flowing secondary, especially when the free safety slides his alignment too far toward the strong side of the offense. The blocking rules for the counteroption are explained in Chapter 1, and as you can see from Diagram 5–7, a fast-flowing fifty team is set up well for the counteroption.

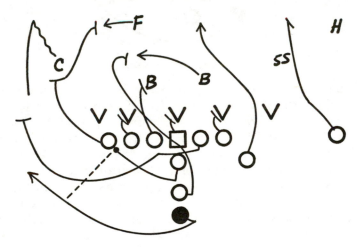

Diagram 5–7

The faking fullback is critical to the success of the counteroption. If he and the quarterback make a good fake, both the inside linebackers will be held up long enough for our blockers to cut off their pursuit. The fullback can effectively block the backside linebacker if he will carry out his fake just as though he has the ball. To do this he will read the block on the frontside linebacker and cut accordingly. On the fake he does the same thing for eight steps downfield. At that point he should be out in front of the backside linebacker and in good position to wall him off from the pitch back. The frontside defensive tackle should read a trap-block, aiding the onside tackle's seal-block. If the offensive tackle will delay an instant, his block will be even easier. If this defender is too strong for the offensive tackle, but will sink if he is aligned to the side of a split end, you can make that adjustment when necessary. This whole concept is explained at length in Chapter 8. Whether the weakside end is tight or split makes no difference to the end, who will follow the same route to get to the free safety from either alignment position. He will release with three flat outside steps if he is tight, or with three flat inside steps if he is wide. Either way the timing of the play is not hampered.

After all the players take the first three steps, this play develops exactly the same as the belly option. This is especially true for the pulling guard, quarterback, and pitchback.

This counteroption is slightly different from the traditional trap option. It is more effective over the long-run because there is no new learning for the quarterback and pulling guard. The traditional trap option requires the quarterback to pivot and read the movement of the defensive tackle, then run a triple option from that read. This requires an athlete who is both mentally and physically superior in the quarterback position. Your blocking scheme should be built on the concept of the fullback blocking the backside linebacker. When he can do this effectively, every other blocker can attack one man closer to the option area, giving the quarterback the same read he gets on the regular belly option.

Another effective maneuver to defeat the overreacting free safety is the counterless counteroption. This approach (Diagram 5-8) gives the defense the impression that the play is going in the direction of the motion. On many plays run from a double-wing set, the action is with the motion. By having your pitch back start in one direction, then pivot back towards his initial alignment on the snap, you get the counter effect. This technique is easily assimilated by the pitch back. Everyone else on the offensive unit executes your normal option play with whatever blocking scheme you desire to use.

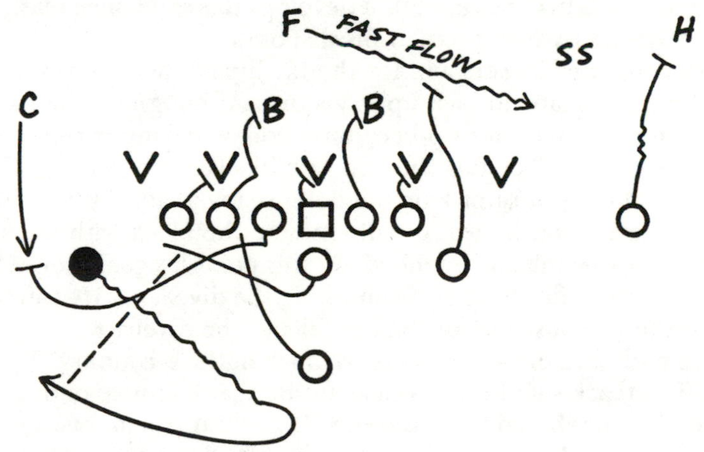

Diagram 5-8

Running Inside

Running outside is always preferable to running inside against the fifty-two. To run outside successfully you must force the defense to honor the inside game. First you run the straight-hitting dive play with man-blocking at the bubble of the defense. By increasing the line splits, additional pressure is placed on each defender near the point of attack. This forces each defender to be responsible for a larger area, giving the blockers an advantage. The ballcarrier need only read the bubble and cut off the blocker's helmet, and the play has a great opportunity for success.

The offensive tackles should be able to turn out their defensive counterpart if they face the standard fifty techniques. Both guards and the center are to block their count man any way they can. Each of the blockers uses the near hip of his assignment as the landmark. Each blocker gets his head to the frontside of the defender and establishes a seam for the ballcarrier. If the defender reads this and pursues quickly to regain outside leverage, a seam should open elsewhere along the line. It is not likely that all the defenders will defeat the blocker's head and regain outside leverage. The diveback will have the seam he seeks if he can spot the blocker that has maintained leverage on the defender. If the blocker feels the defender beating him to the outside, it still may not be a problem if he will stay on the man and ride him in the direction he is moving.

This certainly puts the burden on the ballcarrier. He has to read instantly where the opening is developing. But the ballcarrier is also the one who gets all the publicity when the play breaks, so he had better find the seam if he wants the publicity. Anyone can be a back if his only responsibility is to run straight ahead until he gets hit. We drill the ballcarrier on running to daylight regularly, using our run-to-daylight drill. We place a coach holding a helmet on a large bag and move it to either side when the back is on top of him. The repetition develops this skill; once mastered, the ballcarrier has an excellent tool at his disposal.

By having the blockers aim for the far hip of each interior defender, they are in good shape to pick up any stunt. Although we are calling this man-blocking, it could end up becoming zone-blocking if the count man stunts away and another fills the gap our blocker is entering. When this happens the blocker must pick up the defender who attacks him. When the blocker meets a stunt, he will usually initiate the block with the shoulder opposite to the one initially intended. At this point his goal should be to try and keep the defender he is on from filling the dive lane. He can turn him out or in; the responsibility of the cut falls to the diveback.

Both ends and the slotback are to block in the secondary. The offside end or off-slotback should try to clear inside the defensive end. If he can't clear him, then he should block the end. If he clears them, he will block the free safety or offside cornerback when the offside guard beats him to the free safety. An onside slotback blocks the defensive end to the outside, unless the end will widen with him on an arc release. In that case he can arc to the strong safety and eliminate both defenders.

It is imperative to convince the quarterback and pitchback that a quality fake is integral to the success of the dive. A good fake will often hold the secondary until your blockers get proper leverage. A successful coaching tool is for the head coach to stand facing the backs when they are running a dummy drill. If the backs effectively hide the ball from the coach, then the linebacker who must defeat a block first will have difficulty in locating the ball.

When the noseman is too good to control with straight blocking and the slot lead doesn't satisfy you (Diagram 5–9), try the unbalanced concept. This will force the defense to adjust down and give you different blocking angles. Usually the defense will shift down a full man to the unbalanced. When they do this, you can run the dive with rule blocking. This includes an all important angle-block on the noseman (see Diagram 5–10).

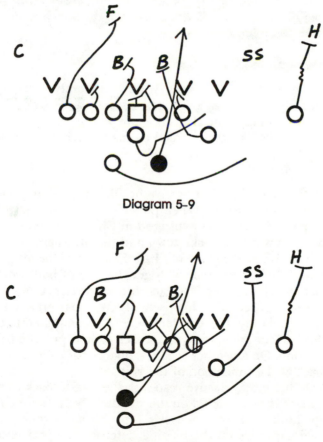

Diagram 5–9

Diagram 5–10

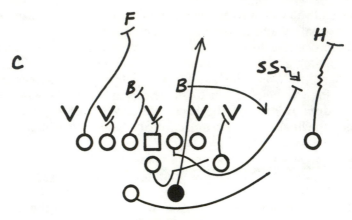

Diagram 5–11

When faced with a linebacker who keys heavily on the pulling guard, it can be advantageous to man-block the dive and false-pull the guard. This can open a very large running lane and destroy the linebacker's confidence in his keys (see Diagram 5–11).

Coaching Point on the Inside Game

When facing a fifty scheme that stunts frequently, you can cheat the dive back closer to the line of scrimmage so the play hits faster. The back will often break clean when he clears the line before the stunt has had time to develop. This must be accompanied by man- or zone-blocking.

Running Off-Tackle

Usually the off-tackle plays versus the fifty-two are extremely important to your offensive success. When possible, start with the rule-blocked outside veer. The blocking was explained in Chapter 1 and shown in Diagram 5–12. Here everyone blocks down and the off guard pulls and leads through the hole. When the angle-blocks are made and the off guard is able to clear the wash before the hole, you get the best of both worlds—every offensive lineman has an angle-block and the ballcarrier comes through the line with a lead blocker. The high-school-level quarterback can handle effectively one read only. If the defensive end is committed to crash hard for the fullback at the snap, the quarterback should pull the ball and run the regular option. On any other read the quarterback should give the ball to the diveback at the conclusion of the ride.

To create the most effective read, ask the quarterback to stay on the ride much longer than he would on the standard belly option. The longer he can keep the ball on the fullback's hip, the more time it buys your blockers to gain leverage on the reading defense. Inexperienced quarterbacks may have success with this play. Also, experiments have been done

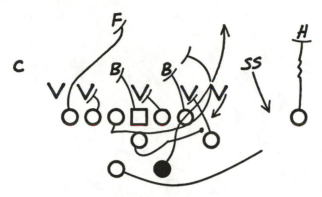

Diagram 5-12

with the quarterback holding the ball just outside the fullback's belly so no fumble will occur because of indecision. Some quarterbacks have found this to be effective, while others feel more comfortable with the standard ride.

When you face a fifty team that stresses control techniques and won't permit your linemen to release inside, or a defense that stunts often, the outside veer must be run with man-blocking. The onside slotback or tight end (if we are going weak side) will combination block with the tackle as described earlier; this will be called man-combo-blocking. The blocking techniques are the same as those used when the inside dive runs with the man-blocking scheme. If they stunt, inside pursuit should be nonexistent, and when your backs are set properly, the off-tackle hole does not lend itself to many stunts from the secondary. When this play is run properly, it looks exactly like the man-blocked dive until the last instant, when the diveback and quarterback slide outside the combination block. If the quarterback is mature, the outside veer can control the game because the offense will have a three-on-two advantage at the corner. A mature defensive end can give a young quarterback a difficult read. But an equally experienced quarterback should be able to focus in on the outside foot of the end to determine handoff or keep.

You want the quarterback to watch the outside foot of the end. When reading a feather-technique end, the quarterback will pull the ball and run the option when the foot comes forward and weight is shifted to it. If the weight is on the inside foot and the outside is back, then the ball should always be given to the diveback.

The outside veer can be run with dive-rule blocking against an opponent that likes to play the defensive end with inside gap-control responsibilities. The tackle will block his count inside and the slotback or tight end will go through for the linebacker. The onside guard will pull and block the end out. This blocking scheme usually suggests a give read, though occasionally the end will close hard, requiring the guard to seal him. In this case the quarterback will bounce outside and run an option. See Diagram 5-13.

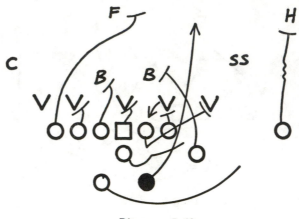

Diagram 5-13

In short yardage situations or whenever else the defensive tackle pinches, your tackle may feel it is easier to block the defender inside. In such a case, the outside veer is run with the complete man-for-man blocking. This eliminates any read on the defensive end. If the guard can stalemate the linebacker, this play should get the yard or two needed for a first down. When you anticipate a crashing defensive end, the blocking will be altered to permit the end or slotback to cross-block the tackle and end. The end or slot will simply call switch-blocking and your tackle will trap the crashing end, usually opening a large hole on an outside angle. This same blocking scheme is especially good when an opponent gives the end-pitch responsibility. It is most effective to the weakside because the free safety cannot provide a quickfill like the strong safety can to his side (see Diagram 5-14). Also it is less likely there will be a stunt by the weakside cornerback and end.

When all of the above conditions are present (tackle and linebacker are inside conscious and the end has pitch), arc-blocking is extremely effective. This places the strong safety directly under the gun. If he fills on the quarterback, the arc pass is wide open; if he honors the arc move of the slotback, the quarterback can roll up through the off-tackle hole behind the fullback or simply give the ball to the fullback, who can follow the arcing slotback.

Against any fifty defense that employs normal outside shoulder techniques while having the end and strong safety stunt at the perimeter on a regular basis, you should use the angle-blocking method with a frontside guard lead. This will compensate for the lack of an arc-block by the slotback. His pull is flat to the line of scrimmage, not deep as in the option. Both the guard and quarterback must read the charge of the defensive end. With the G-lead call made in the huddle, the guard knows from the

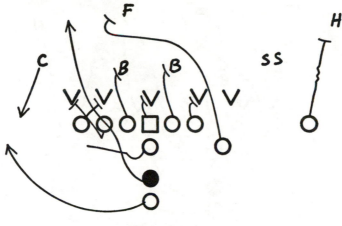

Diagram 5–14

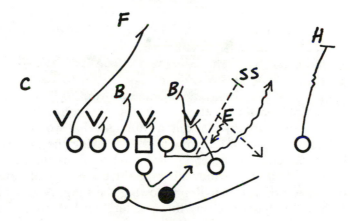

Diagram 5–15

snap that he is to block the strong safety. He must loop outside a pinching end and duck up inside a soft technique or deep-charging end. The quarterback will read the end and give the ball to the fullback if he feathers in the manner described earlier in this section. If the end closes to the inside, the quarterback will pull the ball and run the option behind the pulling guard. In theory, the offense has a two-on-none situation if the split end and slotback make their blocks on the strong safety and strong cornerback as shown in Diagram 5–15.

The final off-tackle possibility against the fifty defense is with the unbalanced line. It is especially good against the team that will not move the defensive front a full man to the long side. Some defenses fear the potential of the shortside game and will only move to an inside control of the next blocker. In this instance, man-block the outside veer. Place the slotback in

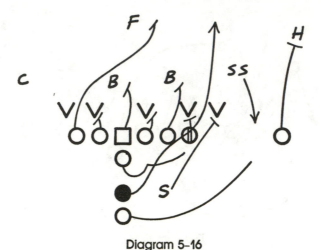

Diagram 5-16

the halfback position; this gives you the threat of the lead dive as well as the loaded option as is shown in Diagram 5-16.

The loaded-blocking scheme is the best way to attack a defensive end that uses different charges. But it is not wise to set the slotback in the halfback position unless he has three linemen in front of him. The unbalanced line provides you with the opportunity to move him into the backfield and not give up any blocking advantages that would have to be yielded in a balanced split-end alignment. By attacking the defensive end from the halfback spot, the defender is forced to show his hand much sooner than he would if he were attacking the slot on the line of scrimmage, who will be engaged on the first step following the snap. Also, by forcing the end to show his hand sooner, the quarterback has an easier read. Sometimes you can encourage the defense to shade their front more toward the short side of the offense by setting the running back on the short-side wing and sending him in motion.

Countering

Counters become an important part of any attack when the backside linebacker flows too quickly or is frequently involved in stunts to the strong side of the offense. Attack this area with the cutback dive and wingback scissor plays. The blocking schemes you use should be determined by the abilities of the defensive tackle and end to that side.

The most basic way to attack this area is with the cutback dive, using man-blocking and having the offside guard and tackle switch assignments. By blocking the guard out, you are protected against an inside control technique often used by a fifty team that wants the offside linebacker to flow quickly. See Diagram 5-17.

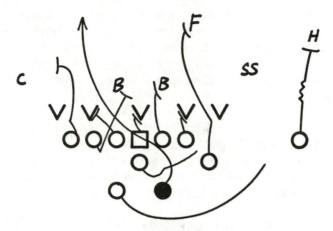

Diagram 5-17

Other fifty teams like to angle their front five toward or away from action on a presnap call or formation key. In these instances, the middle guard can defeat this play if he is slanting the wrong way. You should have success folding both tackles around the guards, who will block out on both defensive tackles. This guarantees that you will seal off the tackle closing to the inside. The folding tackles also have good angles on the inside linebackers, no matter what stunt they use. The problem is the middle guard. It is unfair to ask your center to block a stunting middle guard in a designated direction. But he can wait, get into the middle guard, and ride him in the direction he is slanting. This places the burden on the fullback to cut off the center's block. When the call in the huddle is man-block double-fold, the diveback knows it is his responsibility to cut opposite the slant of the noseman, as shown in Diagram 5-18.

Some angle-fifty teams will develop a definite tendency to angle to the strength of the formation or may possess a middle guard that is too good to

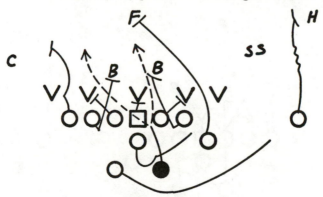

Diagram 5-18

be single-blocked by your center. In this situation it's better to use the cutback dive with the weakside isolation blocking. See Diagram 5–19. This is most effective against angle-fifty teams, which need a monster back to compensate for the void left by the angle. The monster concept prevents them from inverting the secondary and thus permits the split end time to get to the safety.

There is no draw play in the belly option attack, since the passing game is almost all play action. The cutback dive with a running-back lead gives a long yardage inside play. See Diagram 5–20. When you know the pass rush is coming and the linebackers will be dropping, this play works as good as any draw. The blocking scheme is weakside isolation, with the running back designated as the lead blocker instead of the normal slotback lead.

The other counter play is the scissors. This is explained in Chapter 1 and the rule-blocking is shown in Chapter 4. This is the biggest game

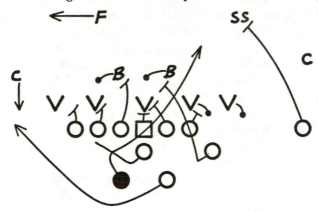

Diagram 5–19

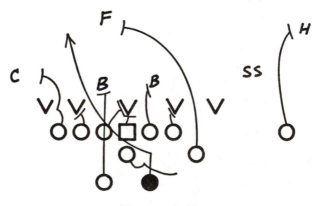

Diagram 5–20

breaker in the offense; use rule-blocking whenever possible. Teams assigning the backside tackle to charge inside your tackle on action away do so in an effort to hamper the game-breaking potential of the scissors. Attack this charge in the same manner as the pinching tackle on the cutback dive. The backside guard and tackle fold-block. Everyone else will rule as always. See Diagram 5-21. The scissors, when used in a long yardage or passing situation with pass- and lead-blocking, is another exemplary method of a draw play without adding such a play. See Diagram 4-18. If there was only one play permitted against the fifty defense, the wingback scissors would be the overwhelming choice of your players year after year.

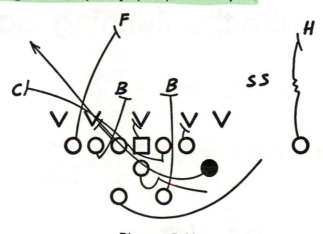

Diagram 5-21

6

How to Attack
the Fifty-Three Battery
with the Running Game

WHEN FACING AN eight-front defense, the passing game should get top priority. But if the offense is to be successful, the belly option offense must be prepared to attack on the ground. Therefore, let's dissect the fifty-three battery.

Strengths of the Fifty-Three Defense

1. With a defensive end and outside linebacker beyond offensive TE/SB, it is strong outside.

2. The three-on-two advantage (DT, OLB, defensive end vs. TE) tackle gives it off-tackle strength.

3. By using an eight-man front as a forcing unit, it is strong versus the running game.

Weaknesses of the Fifty-Three Defense

1. It is a weak defense in the middle with only the middle guard and linebacker aligned on the center and two guards.

2. It is very susceptible to the guard trap.

3. If the outside linebacker (number 3) is aligned off the line, it is weaker off-tackle.

4. With definite areas of responsibility, the three linebackers have only limited pursuit.

5. With only one linebacker (MLB) to protect the hook areas, it is vulnerable to the pass.

Attacking Strategy

1. Run inside with trapping action or man-blocking.
2. Run outside by adjusting the offense to gain a flanking advantage.
3. Run off-tackle when number 2 is forced to defend inside, or by adjusting the offense to gain a blocking advantage off-tackle.
4. Run counterplays behind the flowing middle linebacker.

Running Outside

The alignment of the defensive tackles is the key to determining whether the attack should be run inside or out. If the tackle (number 2) is aligned outside the offensive tackle, it is senseless to try and run wide since there are three defenders over or beyond your tackle. So when the outside running game is discussed, it is assumed that the defensive tackles are in an inside-control technique.

When it has been established that the tackle has dive responsibility and is using an inside control technique, the option play with arc-blocking will become a key part of the attack if they are using zone coverage. The zone usually requires the outside linebacker to take the short arc pass away from the slotback, as shown in Diagram 6–1. If the rest of the line executes man-blocking techniques, the quarterback will be in a good position to read the isolated defensive end for a keep or pitch. If the middle linebacker pursues too quickly for the guard, then the guard and tackle can switch assignments. The guard should scoop-block toward the slanting tackle and the tackle will combo-block toward the middle linebacker as he scrapes off the defensive tackle. To facilitate this block by the guard, he should back off the ball as much as possible; this will permit him more time to gain

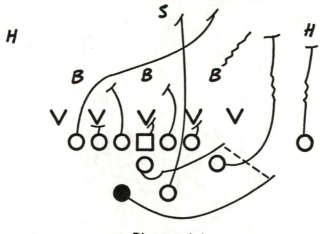

Diagram 6-1

leverage. When the defense doesn't use the outside linebacker to take away the arc pass, that play should become the heart of the attack until an adjustment is made.

Some teams will move the outside linebacker tighter to support the pinching tackle on the wide dive. To compensate for this adjustment, most defenses will slide the free safety over to protect against the arc pass. This requires the offense to make two blocking adjustments. First, all blocks must be straight man-for-man, with the slotback blocking down on the tightened linebacker. Some teams will stack the end and outside linebacker in front of the slotback and game to confuse the slotback. In this situation the slotback should fire at the stack and block the defender that makes the inside move. Second, when the defense moves the free safety over the slotback to take away the arc move, the backfield action should be altered to the wide dive or outside veer. This will provide the fullback a better angle to slide off his fake and work into the face of the free safety, who will be filling fast when the slotback blocks down.

We suggest running opposite a fully rotated free safety using the same blocking scheme. One other possibility to defeat the fully rotated free safety is found in Chapter 3 under play-action passes designed to beat a fast-flowing safety.

If you decide to stay with rule-blocking, some formation adjustments must be made to compensate for the peculiarities of the fifty-three defense. To eliminate the possibility of stunts in the off-tackle area, the split end should be brought in tight and the backfield set strong to the shortside. This will give the offense two alignment advantages. The defense will be outflanked at the off-tackle hole, while the secondary will be shaded toward the wingback until the motion begins. This usually protects the offense from a free safety blitz or rapid fill and gives the frontside blockers a better angle to seal off inside pursuit. Diagram 6–2 shows this play being run from

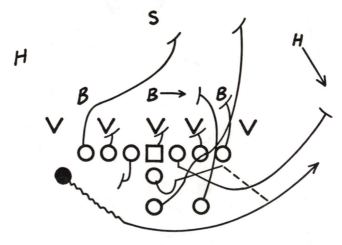

Diagram 6–2

such a formation. A word of caution: though the slotback's assignment remains constant, he must be aware of the onside guard's pull and not delay or he will collide with this puller.

When facing an opponent that has an outstanding nose guard, as is often the case when meeting a fifty-three defense, the option might be run from an unbalanced set. This gives the offense a much easier angle-block on that defender and can negate most of the advantage he had for stunting when he was aligned on the center. Diagram 6–3 shows the option being run from an unbalanced formation. You will note that the unbalanced lineman will block the tackle to his inside after he makes the switch call with the slotback, who will go through for the inside linebacker.

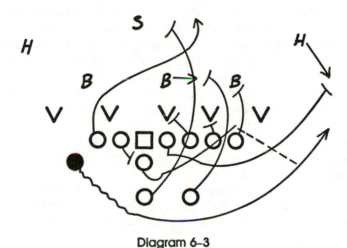

Diagram 6–3

Running Inside

When the defensive tackle sets up in an outside control on the offensive tackle, the inside running game stressing north-south running plays comes to the fore.

The first thing the offense should do is increase the line splits, forcing the nose guard and middle linebacker to cover more territory. The only choice left to the defense is to move the tackles back inside or get ripped apart by the straightahead game.

When attempting to run inside, the middle guard must be given top priority as is done with the middle linebacker in the forty-three defense. On the snap, both the center and offside guard must always take a position step toward the action. They must anticipate a stunt by the middle guard and linebacker. If there is no stunt, the center will aim for position on the frontside hip of the nose guard and take him any way he can. Our centers work on this technique every day. During the daily individual and group periods, the center should always be covered (usually by another center) and should work on handling the various charges in a buddy system. Most of the time you want the helper to work frontside, since this is the toughest block for the center to handle.

The offside guard's first step is toward the center, anticipating a back-side gap stunt. If none develops on the first step, he will charge upfield through the middle linebacker's original position, realizing he will most likely be gone in fast-flow pursuit toward the initial action. If he cannot make contact with the linebacker, he continues upfield toward the safety. The onside guard is in good position to wall off the middle linebacker when he steps to meet the dive. Both tackles have an easy but important assignment. They must wall off their count man, who presumably has outside control responsibility. The tight end and slotback have a similar responsibility with their count man (the third player out from the center). If the outside linebacker's count will step with them, then an outside arc release will be sufficient to eliminate these defenders from quick inside support. If they will not honor the arc move, they must be turned out the same as the tackles. As long as the defensive tackle will not adjust back to the inside of the offensive tackle, the inside running game is the order of the day. The biggest danger is to start overcoaching when there is no need to do anything until the defense adjusts.

If the defensive tackle makes an inside adjustment, the dive can still be run with basically the same blocking. However, it will hit outside the offensive tackle. The slotback or tight end must block the number 3 defender, since the play will bounce wider when the diveback cuts off his tackle's helmet key. Though this play looks just like the outside veer play, it is not; there is no quarterback read. See Diagram 6-4.

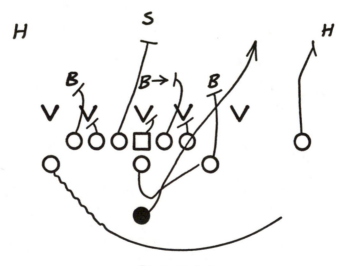

Diagram 6-4

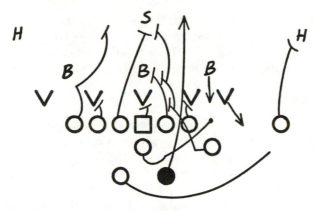

Diagram 6-5

In short yardage situations the dive play has been run effectively with isolation blocking, as is shown in Diagram 6-5. What aids this blocking scheme is the defense's effort to apply quick pressure. Usually the outside linebacker and end will crowd the line of scrimmage and penetrate on the snap. This eliminates the outside linebacker from quick pursuit on the dive. All the linemen follow man-for-man blocking principles and the slotback aligns slightly deeper to gain a good blocking angle on the middle linebacker or middle guard. He will be assigned to help on the most dangerous of the two. If his assignment stunts to the far side of the center, the slotback should continue downfield and block the safety.

Some teams will constantly stunt the middle guard and inside linebacker. If they become a problem, the unbalanced line dive with rule-blocking usually serves as a good antidote. The unbalanced line forces the defense to adjust over a man to prevent being outflanked, and at the same time it provides the offensive onside linemen good angles to seal off any frontside stunt by either of these two defenders. See Diagram 6-6. If the

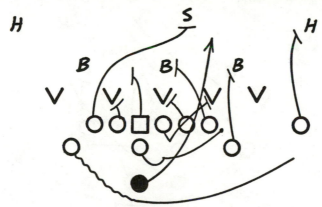

Diagram 6-6

defensive tackle is inclined to use an inside charge, then the slotback and unbalanced guard can switch assignments. This blocking adjustment can also be effective from the tight halfback position when the conditions are similar to those of the previous dive.

Running Off-Tackle

When a fifty-three team becomes too inside-conscious and they move both the tackle (number 2) and the outside linebacker (number 3) to an inside control, the off-tackle game will become an effective weapon. This situation is not often present except on short yardage downs when the defense is trying to jam up all the gaps. The outside veer is the first choice to attack this area. It will hit the same as the man-blocked dive shown in Diagram 6–4, except the quarterback will read the reaction of the defensive end. It can be one of those rare moments that make you feel you're a great coach if you get your quarterback a three-on-one advantage at the corner. The diveback will usually get the ball because the end is usually assigned pitch responsibility. If the fullback can clear the line of scrimmage, he should angle toward the sideline behind the block of the split end. This usually puts him in a foot race with the free safety.

As always, the alignment of the free safety plays an important part in determining the direction of this play. Fifty-three teams often play man-for-man coverage when they are trying to fill all the gaps. When the safety is cheated all the way to the slotback, our philosophy dictates run to the short side. When this alignment is present there is no chance of a secondary stunt from the weakside; this leaves the weakside end and halfback in a very difficult position. The halfback is needed for support as soon as he reads when the tight end is blocking down on the linebacker. But this still gives the quarterback a three-on-two advantage. If the end takes the full-

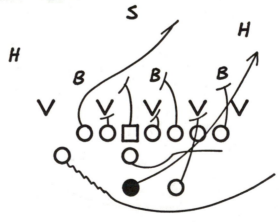

Diagram 6–7

back, the halfback will have his choice of the quarterback or pitchman and by properly splitting the slotback, there should be little hope of the free safety offering immediate aid.

Another strong short yardage play in the off-tackle area is to align in an unbalanced line with the split end tight and backfield set in the wing T to the short side. The motion of the running back will occupy the free safety, while the deep set slotback can serve as a lead blocker on either the tackle or end, helping to ensure the fullback clearing the line of scrimmage. The slotback can also be used to double team a strong middle guard or middle linebacker. See Diagram 6–7.

Countering

When the defense has great confidence in the interior people and lets them play straight up football without relying on interior stunting, the counters become an important facet of the option attack.

The first counter play to be considered is the cutback dive. Usually the middle linebacker will flow quickly to meet the first threat and the middle guard will give slow-read pursuit. The linebacker recognizes the dive blocking scheme and overpursues the onside guard, who will fire-out as he does on the dive and let the linebacker use his own momentum to carry himself outside the frontside guard. The middle guard is usually responsible for stopping the inside cutback, so double-team him by either bringing the backside guard or tackle down. If you seal with the guard and the defensive tackle shuffles down instead of penetrating, the play will be forced so far to the backside it will go nowhere. The safest blocking scheme is to angle the guard out on the tackle to ensure a seal to the weak side and pull the tackle toward the middle stack. The center can single-block the noseman toward the frontside, but if he is unsuccessful, the offside tackle will wall him off with a trap block. Ideally, the middle guard will have flowed to the frontside, and the tackle can turn upfield seeking the first opponent to show, looking first for the middle linebacker, who may be involved in a middle stunt to the backside, and then to the free safety. As always, wide line splits are critical to opening the interior running lanes. The backside tackle should align as far off the ball as possible to give himself a better angle to read and assess the action over the middle (Diagram 6–8).

The second counter play that has proven most successful against the fifty-three is the double dive. This play has been the biggest statistical gainer in the option attack over the years against this defense. The blocking is straight man-for-man, which results in a double-team on the middle linebacker and a single-block on the middle guard. The idea is to let the fast-flowing superior noseman attack the diveback, then send both guards on the cautious middle linebacker, who is probably reading the pitchback. The noseman will run himself out of the play and the tailback will cut behind him. He will then cut off the double-team block on the linebacker. He can

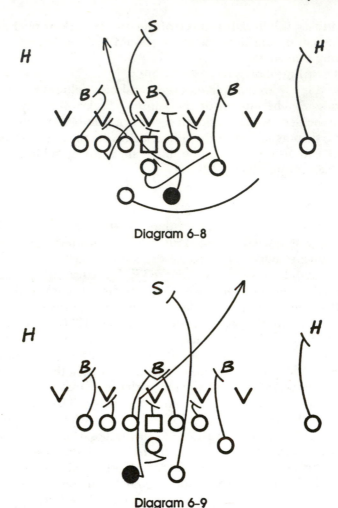

Diagram 6-8

Diagram 6-9

cut to the frontside and slide in behind the fullback's block on the safety. Your first reaction to Diagram 6-9 is that the middle guard will tackle the fullback. But in most cases that player will realize by about the second step that he's been had, and will put all his effort into trying to get back in pursuit, leaving the fullback to pass through the line untouched.

The scissors counter must be kept on the front burner against the fifty-three defense. It has always been the option's bread and butter, the "keep them honest" play that is especially good when both the middle people are superior players.

The primary blocking scheme is always the first choice. That blocking method was described in Chapter 1. The backside shows pass to encourage the offside tackle and end to rush, while the tight end seals off the middle linebacker. The frontside guard will pull and lead through on the corner

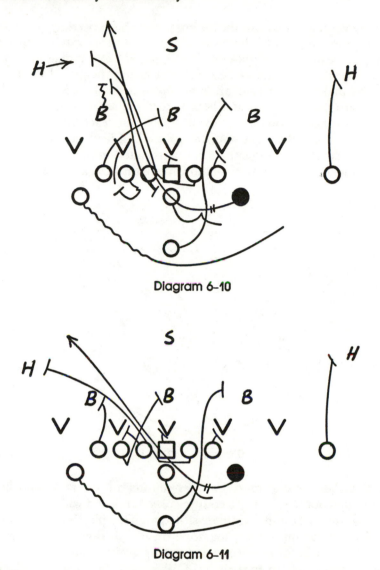

Diagram 6-10

Diagram 6-11

linebacker. If the end rushes deep, the offside guard will not block him but will get on track and block the cornerback, leaving the backside halfback for the second guard through. When this happens it is usually a touchdown. This blocking method is shown in Diagram 6-10.

When the backside defensive tackle is playing a control technique and is not concerned with rapid-pass rush, the tight end side can switch assignments to ensure success. The guard will block out on the tackle to seal off his pursuit, while the tight end will turn out the corner linebacker and his middle linebacker responsibility will be taken by the tackle on a fold-block. See Diagram 6-11.

In long yardage situations the defense might be expecting a counter as an alternative to the pass. In these situations, the scissors can be run with a complete pass read by the tight-end side. The tight end makes an outside pass release, pushing off the weakside halfback, and the guard to that side will take the middle linebacker after he shows a pass-block. The pulling guard will turn a tight corner and look to lead the scissors straight up the field. His first concern will be the corner linebacker reacting inside. If that defender drops with the tight end, the guard will lead down to the free safety. This was the play and situation that resulted in the winning touchdown for Widener in the 1981 National Championship game. See Diagram 6–12.

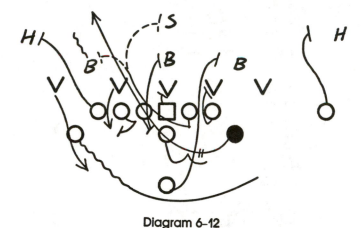

Diagram 6–12

Finally, there is one more counter-counter play that should be included. Though not necessarily a counter play, it is listed with the counters because it is usually run in a counter situation. This play has proven most successful when run in the scoring zone on fourth down and long. The defense will often be in man coverage, trying to exert some type of gap pressure. In this situation the scissors-fake-option with man-blocking can be a stunning success. The free safety should flow with the slotback. The outside linebacker will read counter also and start to slide to the inside. When this occurs, the quarterback usually gets the desired two-on-one at the corner. He will probably keep the ball when the end overcommits on the pitchback, leaving no one to take the quarterback. See Diagram 6–13.

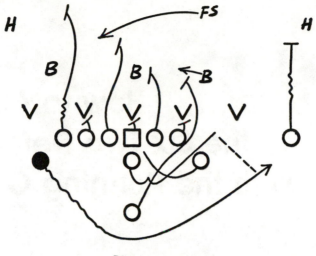

Diagram 6-13

7

How to Attack
the Six-Two Defenses
with the Running Game

THE SIX-TWO or four-four type defenses, although eight-front defenses like the five-three, still present problems in regard to attacking the various looks when compared to the odd front.

Strengths of the Six-Two Defenses

1. These defenses are strong against the option when the number 3 defender aligns outside the tight end or slotback.
2. The split-six is strong over the middle since there are four defenders aligned over three offensive players, while the wide tackle and regular six are both strong off-tackle to the outside.
3. They are good pursuit defenses because of the four-linebacker concept.
4. They are good stunting defenses with many possibilities.

Weaknesses of the Six-Two Defenses

1. When the tight end flexes from 5 feet to 4 yards, the split-six off-tackle area becomes vulnerable as the area defended by number 3 is stretched to the limit. The wide six and regular six are weak inside with just two down linemen versus the two offensive guards and center.
2. Quick hitters are effective since there are often only four linemen.
3. If the tackles are not physically superior, the whole defense becomes vulnerable.

4. If the outside linebackers can be sealed in, these defenses are very weak against the option.

5. Proper adjustments are critical if these defenses are to remain sound.

Attacking Strategy

1. Run directly at these defenses with man- or trap-blocking.

2. Force number 4 to declare for run or pass.

3. Counter fast-flowing backside inside linebackers.

Attacking the Outside

To be able to run outside effectively against the six-two defense, the number 3 defender must play an inside technique on the slot or tight end. As long as he plays an outside control, the defense has too many people with outside leverage and the option pitch threat is minimized. When this situation is present it is usually necessary to open the game with several dives to encourage the number 3 man to move inside. By so doing, he can take away the down block on his inside defender and he can also tackle the ballcarrier.

Once the number 3 defender moves to the (7 technique alignment) inside shoulder of the slot, it becomes advantageous to run the option. To further ensure success on the guard pull option, the offense can create additional complications for the defense, forcing them to make more adjustments. By locating the tight end about 12 yards beyond his normal position, the safety will be forced to cheat deeper so he can protect the deep third on any zone type of rotation. This will prevent the safety from being able to offer the forcing unit any quick-run support. On the other side of the formation, the split end can close his split around 4 yards to place additional pressure on the number 3 defender.

Either he or the number 4 defender must now revert to a position off the line of scrimmage to take away the leverage advantage gained by flexing the end. The defense could counteract the threat of the tightened slot by rotating the secondary to that side. But if the running back is placed in the slot position inside the split tight end, the defense cannot as easily make this adjustment. To execute an option, the running back is placed in a short motion just prior to the snap and the players to the strong side will block down to the inside as shown in Diagrams 7–1, 7–2, and 7–3.

If the number 3 defender aligns inside the slotback, he becomes the slotback's block. The flexed split end will go through to the inside linebacker. This buys considerable time for the quarterback as he tries to run the option on number 4.

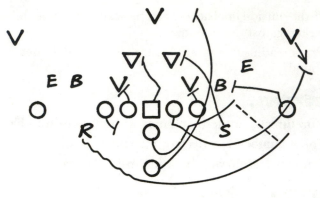

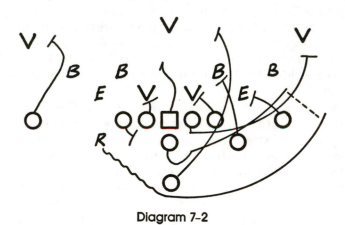

Diagram 7-1

Diagram 7-2

Diagram 7-3

Problems with the Option

1. If the defensive end charges hard on the snap, he can prevent the pitch. Of course, the quarterback keep and the dump pass to either the split end or slotback becomes a serious threat to this defense once they sacrifice their flat soundness.

2. If the six-two has a superior athlete at the number 3 linebacker position, he will more than likely be able to take the pitch away from the option team. In this case, the offense must either run to the opposite side or try some other approach of attack.

3. If the split-six defense is strong at the inside linebacker positions, it is usually hard to fold block them. If you know you will be facing superior athletes at this spot, you will not want to spend much time that week working on a blocking technique that will more than likely result in failure on game day.

Running Inside

When playing against the six-two defenses, we have always favored the belly dive in the running game strategy. Since these are basically gap types of defenses, the offensive blockers are given many good angles to establish their blocks.

The dive can be blocked several different ways. The type of blocking favored will be determined by the alignment of number 3. If he is aligned in an outside shade, presumably to keep himself free to control the quarterback on the option, then it is preferable to run the dive with rule-trap-blocking. See Diagrams 7–4, 7–5, and 7–6. If the number 3 defender is aligned in an inside shade, preferring to concentrate on keeping the slot or tight end off the linebacker, the play is best blocked by folding the guard

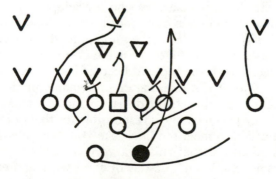

Diagram 7–4

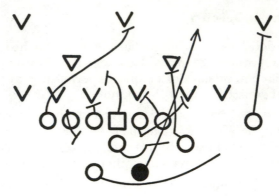

Diagram 7-5

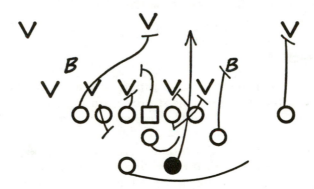

Diagram 7-6

around the tackle to the linebacker versus the split or wide, while arcing the slot or tight end to the safety. See Diagrams 7-7 and 7-8.

The arc-blocking method can also be amended further if the defense possesses especially sharp linebackers who are adept at beating the fold technique. In this situation the scoop-block is good. The guard will reach-block to the far hip of the tackle; at the same time, the slot tackle will step directly to the outside hip of the defensive tackle to prevent any outside loop. When the tackle feels the hip and head of his guard swing alongside of him, he will continue up field and attempt to maintain his outside leverage on the scraping linebacker. If the defensive tackle is making an outside move, then the tackle becomes solely responsible for that defender and the guard will step upfield to meet the linebacker filling inside this tackle.

It is not hard to see that this is a very complex technique and is something that is not put in on Tuesday of game week and expected to be successful on Saturday. It is a technique that must be developed over a long period of time. Therefore, you must determine in the off-season if you

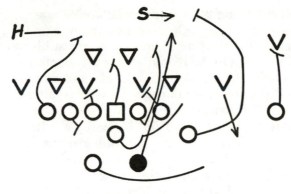

Diagram 7–7

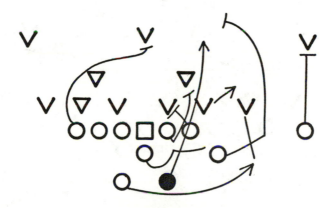

Diagram 7–8

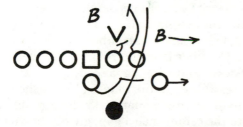

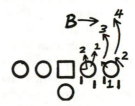

Diagram 7–9

expect to face this maneuver in the fall. If you think that the scoop-block will be needed frequently, it should be included in the teaching segment of each practice from the first day of fall practice. On the other hand, if you believe that your people are good enough to survive with just the trap and fold blocks, this extra blocking scheme can be avoided. See Diagram 7–9.

If the fullback is the strength of the offensive running game and has good quickness and reactions, the read dive can be a strong running play. This is especially effective if the fullback is better at his position than the pulling guard is at his. On the read dive versus the split-six, the guard and tackle will double-team the defensive tackle and attempt to drive him straight back off the line of scrimmage. This will create a conjection problem for the scrape linebacker. He will be forced to react quickly to the inside or outside of the double-team. In most cases he will scrap to the outside of the tackle and the quarterback will give the ball to the fullback slightly deeper. The fullback will run at the double-team and read the flow of the linebacker. When the linebacker makes his decision to fill inside or outside, the fullback will cut to the opposite side of the double-team. See Diagram 7–10. The rest of the line's blocks are easier to complete since every blocker has a good angle of attack.

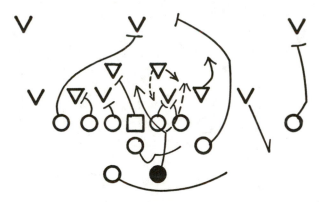

Diagram 7–10

Note the center's block against the split-six. He should step on gap first to stop a fast blitz by the onside linebacker. This defender could, with fast penetration, stop the play before it gets started. If no blitz shows, then the center continues on to the offside linebacker and either seals him to the offside or takes him straight on. In either case the fullback can become adept at reading the onside linebacker and running accordingly.

Another variation that is successful versus the wide-six look is the lead dive with two blocking adjustments. The onside guard takes a large split to entice the number 1 defender into the center-guard gap, giving the guard an angle-block on that defender. The tackle blocks out on the number 3 defender and the slotback leads on the linebacker aligned in the number 2 position. See Diagram 7–11.

Whichever of these various blocking methods you decide to use, you must also consider the abilities of all of the offensive and defensive personnel. *You always want to attack the defense's weakest people with your strongest.*

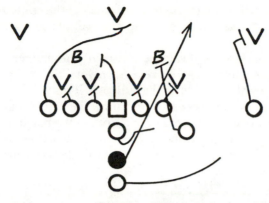

Diagram 7-11

These various blocking schemes permit the belly option to attack the six-two dive area often and successfully during the course of any game.

Running Off-Tackle

If the number 3 defender declares to the inside of the slotback, the offense is given angle-blocks all the way down the line. At this point it is to the offense's advantage to run the outside-veer attack inside number 4. All the offensive blockers should block to the inside using man-for-man principles. The quarterback will ride the fullback to the outside of number 3, requiring the contain man to play either the fullback, quarterback, or pitch. This is the ideal situation, assuming all the blockers can sustain their blocks.

If the number 3 defender is of superior ability and neither the slotback nor the tight end can effectively block him, then the blocking should be changed to arc-option-blocking (see Diagram 7-12); when using the option arc the quarterback must read number 4. If number 4 chases the

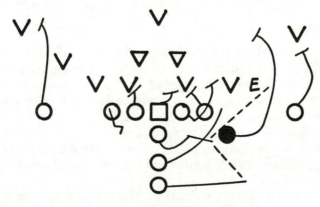

Diagram 7-12

arcing slotback, he will pitch to the trailing back. If the contain man honors the pitch, the quarterback should dump the ball off to the slotback as he arcs upfield.

The quarterback must always be aware of the danger of quick pressure from numbers 3 and 4. As he reverse pivots, the ball should be held high when he comes off the ride of the fullback. This will allow him to have a quick release if it becomes necessary to dump the ball off early. If he rides the fullback in the normal manner, he will not get the ball into the throwing position fast enough to execute an accurate pass. Also, there is great danger of having the pass batted down when he tries to deliver what usually ends up a low trajectory throw.

The other choice is to run the outside veer of the end-wing. This ensures the seal-block on number 3 via the double-team and still provides a three-on-two advantage (fullback-quarterback-pitchback versus defenders numbers 4 and 5). See Diagram 7–13.

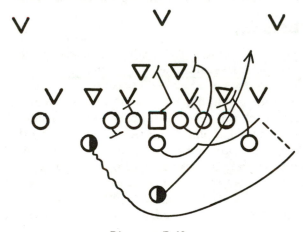

Diagram 7–13

Countering

The split-six by design has numerical advantages inside the offensive tackles. Therefore, to counter inside, the offensive team must force movement from the inside linebackers. Also, the various six-two's usually are pressure types of defenses, so any slow developing counters will always have a low performance ratio unless you are able to accurately determine when the defense will not be running in a stunt.

Because of these features of the six-two defenses, it is best to run quick-hitting counters. Fullback counters off the dive action are the surest plays in this situation.

One of the best fullback counters is the inside veer back by the fullback. It is designed to hit behind the scraping linebacker. In this play both guards must turn out on the pinching tackles and the center will wall off the linebacker that scrapes to action. The key to this play against the split-six is the method used by the two tackles to block the offside linebacker, who is responsible for handling any inside counters. The onside tackle will pull to trap him if he blitzes. If there is no blitz, then the tackle will turn up into the hole after the linebacker. If the linebacker is already blocked by the farside tackle, he will continue upfield to the safety. The farside tackle will release upfield after the same linebacker. If the linebacker blitzes, then the tackle should turn straight upfield and attack the safety. The timing of this block is not as complicated as it appears on paper. The movement of the linebacker makes the decision of the tackles relatively easy. See Diagrams 7–14a and 7–14b.

   This scheme is also used versus the wide-six and the regular six if the offensive guards can block the two number 1 defenders.

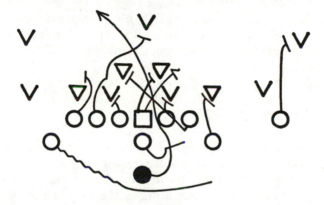

Diagram 7–14a

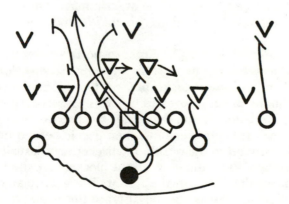

Diagram 7–14b

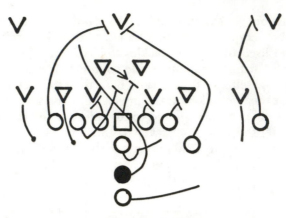

Diagram 7-15

Another effective blocking scheme for this play versus the split-six is the guard-tackle fold block (Diagram 7–15). This method is especially valuable when the linebackers read flow and scrape. The fold block can be effective since the linebacker protecting the middle usually does not see the folding linebacker until too late.

The belly option's most effective counter, the scissors trap, is good only when the offense is sure they will not see any unusual stunt. As you can see from Diagrams 7–16, 7–17, and 7–18, if any of the defenders blitz, it can create havoc in the offensive backfield. But if the defense can be caught playing the basic look, this play should be a game breaker. One blocking adjustment is required against the number 3 technique tackle in the split-six defense. The onside tackle must be the puller instead of the guard. If the guard pulls, the penetrating tackle would always stop the play before it could get started.

The blocking scheme shown in Diagram 7–14 has been successful when instead of working back to the sideline, the slotback turns the play straight upfield after he crosses the line of scrimmage. On all scissors plays, the fullback is responsible for filling on the defender with quarterback responsibility.

If you are going to face an opponent who favors pressure from the front and backsides while letting the two inside linebackers flow freely, use the blocking scheme shown in Diagram 7–19, but be cautioned that all of the above conditions must be present for this to be considered a high-consistency play. Both guards and the onside tackle have easy cutoff blocks. The center lets the off linebacker flow, then gets in behind him. The far-side tackle pulls through to the onside linebacker, who usually never sees him until it is too late. Unfortunately, all the blockers are used up blocking the forcing unit. In this situation the scissors is a good play to get a first down. But it will seldom break for the distance since you are not blocking anyone in the defensive secondary.

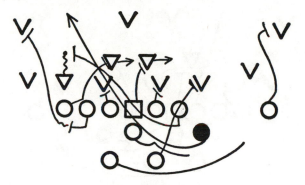

Diagram 7-16

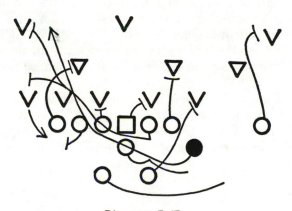

Diagram 7-17

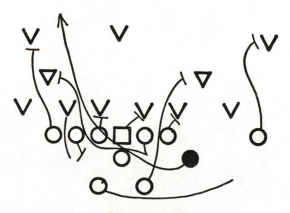

Diagram 7-18

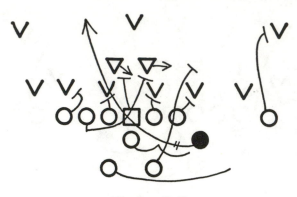

Diagram 7-19

In conclusion, it is important to remember that this chapter deals only with the running-game attack of the six-two defenses. Since these are eight-front defenses stressing the use of pressure, refer back to Chapter 3 to get the complete picture on attacking the defense. The biggest weakness in these defenses is in the under coverage, when the linebackers are used for pressure. Much of what you want to accomplish against this defense will be found in Chapter 3.

The easiest way to determine if you should run or pass on the six-two defense is to check the alignment of number 4. If he is on the line of scrimmage, the defense are heavily committed to run support and you should seriously consider passing. If he is aligned off the line of scrimmage, it is more advisable to run at the soft corner.

8

How to Attack the Off-Set Gap Defense with the Running Game

ONE OF THE MORE recent trends in defensive football is in the area of off-set defenses. This scheme lends itself well to the fifty concept. The off set wants to take advantage of lateral field position or certain advantages provided by offensive formations. Many colleges are changing to this style of defense in an effort to stop the various option attacks. This thinking has filtered down to the high-school level and is beginning to play a big part in planning at that level.

To effectively attack the off set, you must be extremely conscious of the over-shifted alignment. Knowing how an opponent proposes to set this over-shift will have an important bearing on where it should be attacked. The basic double-tight set explained in Chapter 1 discourages most off-set gap adjustments, since these defenses are primarily designed for offenses using a pro-type look. The defense will slide away from the split end. The following diagrams are three examples of off-set defenses (see Diagram 8–1).

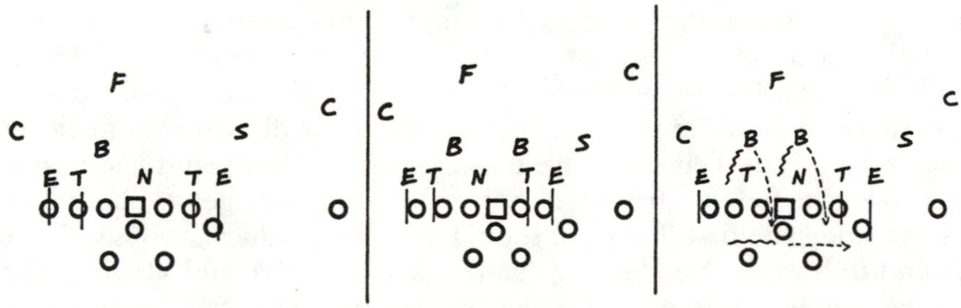

Diagram 8–1

Strengths of the Off-Set Gap Defense

1. The stacks in the gaps are good for blitzing.
2. It is strong toward direct action because all the gaps will be covered.
3. The stacks and off-sets have a tendency to create blocking confusion.
4. It provides the linebackers with good run support opportunities.

Weaknesses of the Off-Set Gap Defense

1. It is weak off-tackle to the downshifted side.
2. It lacks good pursuit angles outside to the downshifted side.
3. It is not a balanced defense.
4. It provides poor under coverage vs. play-action passes.

Attacking Strategy

1. Due to the off-set gap concept there are several good angles for trapping inside.
2. Counters and counteroptions are good opposite the linebacker's fill.
3. Use motion to change strength and defeat the basic premise of the off-set gap defense.

Running Outside

Anytime you see an unbalanced defense your first instinct should be to attack at the short side of the defense. The counteroption was added to the belly attack for this specific purpose. There are good blocking angles on all the down linemen and the threat of the fullback trap holds the linebackers long enough for the blockers to gain leverage on them. You will note from Diagram 8-2 that there is only one block that requires any degree of skill; that is the block on the frontside linebacker. This block gets easier after a couple of successful fullback traps have been run inside of him. In fact, this defense provides the belly option with such good blocking angles that you should try to force teams to make the downshift adjustment if you know it is in their defensive package. Most offset teams like to sink (close down the defense from the short side) when they get a split end on the weak side. The first thing you should do to help achieve this is split the tight end to 8 yards. No blocking changes are required, and the tight end does not change any aspect of his blocking assignment except by running a different route to get back on his blocking course. See Diagram 8-3.

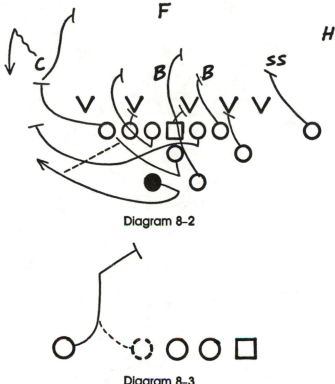

Diagram 8-2

Diagram 8-3

Using the same line of reasoning, go unbalanced to run the belly option play. Since this is an unbalanced defense, the easiest way to achieve balance would be to use an unbalanced offense to negate any advantage gained by the defensive alignment. When you go unbalanced against an opponent that plays an off-set gap stack, you can usually eliminate any choice on how they will slide their line. They must slide to the offensive long side. Also, if the running back is set on the wing, the defense cannot roll up the secondary to the long side. The ability of the center to reach-block the noseman is critical to the onside blocking scheme. If he can stop the noseman's penetration, it frees the slotback to be set either in the halfback position or as a wingback. Move the slotback around to defeat the various defensive-end techniques. For example, if the end is responsible for controlling the last man on the line of scrimmage, the slot can either align as a halfback and execute a load block on him or align in the slot position to ensure an easy release by your tackle to the linebacker. If the end is not playing a control technique, the slotback can be aligned in a position that will aid in setting up some other play in the game plan. See Diagram 8-4.

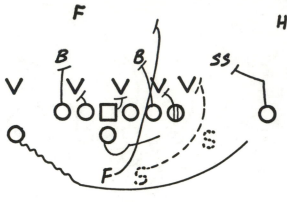

Diagram 8-4

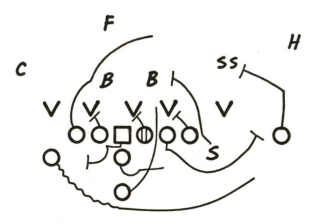

Diagram 8-5

When you face an outstanding noseman capable of beating the center's reach-block, alter the unbalanced procedure slightly and place the shifting guard next to the center instead of outside the splitside tackle. When this adjustment is made, the slotback must align in his normal position. This gives you enough people along the front to block everyone on the inside of the defense. See Diagram 8-5.

When the free and strong safety fully rotate to the strong side of the offense, the directional rules explained in Chapter 4 come into play. It becomes advantageous to run the belly option (or the trap option) to the short side. When the free safety cannot give quick support at the perimeter, your fullback should be able to wall him off as he pursues across the field. See Diagram 8-6. Also, if the free safety has adjusted to the strong side beyond the position of the center or will make that adjustment when you use motion, it is worthwhile to run the belly option to the short side even if

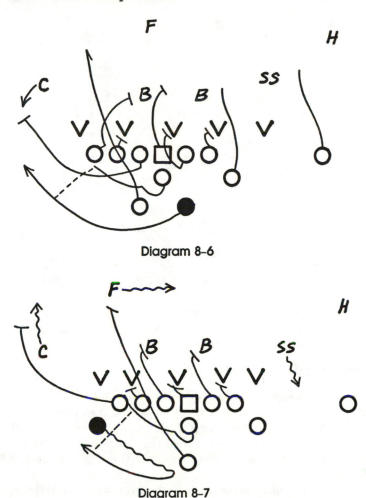

Diagram 8-6

Diagram 8-7

the line is shaded as shown in Diagram 8–7. In this situation arc-blocking is best since they have four linemen to the side you are attacking and the quick stalemate sometimes provides the best results (see Chapter 6).

When the offset gap defense uses the strong safety as a contain end, you have created problems for the defense by adjusting to a false unbalanced line by using jet motion. To jet: The slotback is placed on the line of scrimmage instead of his normal depth of 1 yard. The tight end will never touch his hand to the ground when he aligns in his normal position and will also stand slightly deeper than normal. On the quarterback's foot signal he goes in motion to the split side. His assignment is to turn back on the first pursuit from the inside (usually the offside linebacker). There are no rule changes for the rest of the team. When you run the option with this block-

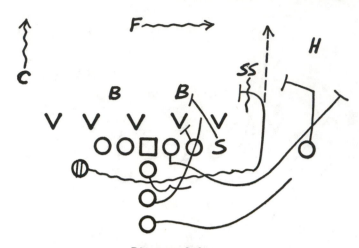

Diagram 8-8

ing scheme, the tight-end-arc pass is an outstanding complementary play. This action places the strong safety in a real bind. He must contain the pitch on the option, but is also responsible for the short pass zone under the free safety. By mixing these plays the belly can eliminate any prospects of a fully rotated secondary. See Diagram 8-8.

Running Inside

Running inside is very difficult due to the nature of the off-set gap defense. They are in the gaps at the snap and can get quick penetration, while the linebackers are only a step from a gap to either side and are able to quickly seal up the nature bubbles of the defense. We have found only one inside running play is consistent against this defense, and that is the lead dive.

We favor the unbalanced concept to encourage the defensive line to shade to our best advantage. The slotback is aligned in a halfback position and the running back is set on the wing. This discourages the defense from prerotating the secondary. The belly dive play can be a consistent gainer when you use an isolation blocking scheme. The lead blocker on the linebacker will be the slotback. See Diagram 8-9 and refer back to Chapter 1 for the blocking variations on the lead dive. You will note that the unbalanced guard still blocks his basic man-blocking assignment. To complete this block he should fold through the hole behind the split-side tackle. There are times when he will end up running into the onside linebacker and end up on a double team with the leading slotback. This often happens when the defense is playing the gap-stack type of off-set. But this is not as big a problem as you might imagine, since the double-team often walls off the pursuing backside linebacker. See Diagram 8-10.

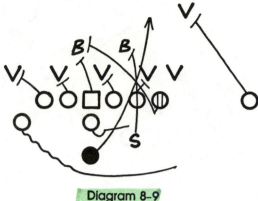

Diagram 8-9

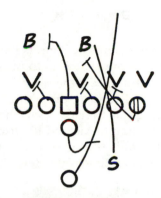

Diagram 8-10

Running Off-Tackle

The off-tackle area presents the best possibilities for establishing an inside running attack, since only one player is assigned responsibility for that area. Your best play is the outside veer. Run the play toward the off-set. In Diagram 8-11 you can see the fine blocking angles provided each blocker. The tackle has the responsibility of filling this area. But if the defensive tackle does a good job of holding up the offensive tackle, you cannot get a good block on the frontside backer. This permits him to flow cleanly into the off-tackle hole and stop the wide veer. To counteract this defensive maneuver, have your tackle switch assignments with the slotback to prevent the linebacker from filling cleanly in the off-tackle area. When the defensive tackle is so conscious of controlling the onside tackle's release to the linebacker, it becomes easy for the blocker to get a good piece of the defender.

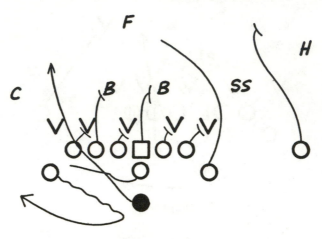

Diagram 8-11

This blocking adjustment is not without its dangers. Major problems can develop when you face a team that likes to blitz this linebacker inside the defensive tackle. If this stunt occurs when a switch stunt is called, the linebacker will come clean and destroy the play. When this possibility is present, do not permit your tackle to make a switch call. In this situation, a combination type of block on the tackle and linebacker is the only adjustment the offense can make. This is a hard technique to develop, since it requires timing and an understanding of the defense by the two key offensive blockers.

If you have great confidence in the blocking of the slotback or tight end, this play can be run away from the off-set as shown in Diagram 8-12.

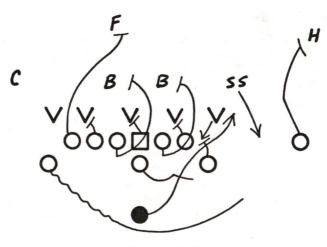

Diagram 8-12

By using man-for-man blocking, both tackles and the center have good blocking angles but the guards should fold to the linebacker. The key to the success of this play is in the ability of the slot or tight end to control the defensive end aligned inside or over him. If this player cannot be controlled, then this play will never gain an inch.

The third choice and often the best method of running the outside veer is to use regular dive-rule blocking while running the play away from the off-set as shown in Diagram 8-13. Now everyone has fine blocking angles and if the offside will reach block, they can pick up any interior stunts. The tight end or slotback has a great angle on the scrape linebacker, leaving the defensive end with a tremendous gap to cover while he tries to seal off the fullback dive and slow the quarterback.

No matter which of these three off-tackle plays you select, be sure you include the off-tackle attack as part of the game plan in defeating the off-set gap defense.

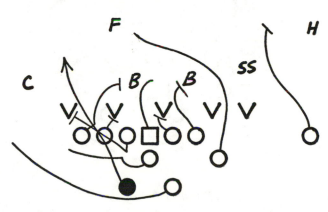

Diagram 8-13

Countering

As stated earlier, running inside directly at the off-set gap defense is not a strong percentage way to move the football, but countering this defense with its flowing linebackers is definitely advised.

The counter dive or fullback-cutback dive are good choices against this defense. Run the counter dive away from the off-set as shown in Diagram 8-14. Each offensive blocker has a good angle except for the backside tackle. The key to this blocking scheme is determined by the tackle's ability to wall off that defender. If the linebacker fills quickly and cannot be sealed off by the tackle, use man-blocking with a fold by the onside tackle and guard as seen in Diagram 8-15. Again, each blocker has a good angle and the tackle is in great position to seal off the linebacker if he is good at scraping into the counter area.

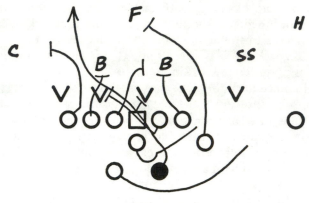

Diagram 8–14

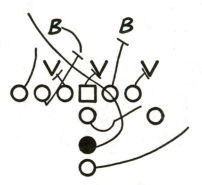

Diagram 8–15

Though the scissors is considered the biggest game breaker in the belly option offense, we are not anxious to use this play against the off-set gap defense. The logic is obvious. This defense favors quick hitting counters, so a slow-developing play like the scissors becomes a low-consistency play. But this play is always so popular with the players that you may be forced to include it in your game plan, even though there may be times when you are convinced it is not in your best interest to do so.

If you decide to include the scissors, run it from the wing-slot formation to get a favorable secondary adjustment. The action of the series will be toward the weak side of the off-set and the counter scissors will hit back to the strength of the defense. In Diagram 8–16 you can see the fine influence-blocking angles presented the guard and tackle. If the linebacker flows to action, he is vulnerable to the down block of the tight end. The running-back motion gets the secondary revolving in the desired direction, setting up a potentially great counter. When you face a team that does not blitz the linebackers, the scissors can maintain a high consistency game-

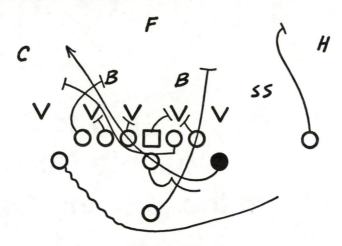

Diagram 8-16

breaking average. But if you run the scissors when the linebackers are blitzing straight ahead, the play is doomed. And by nature, the off-set gap defense is a stunting defense.

Be sure to refer back to Chapter 3 when preparing for this style of defense. Since the linebackers are so conscious of filling unprotected gaps, they are usually poor at covering the hook-and-curl passing zones. By combining counters and short passes behind the linebackers, this popular style of defense can play right into your hands.

9

How to Attack Multiple Defenses with the Running Game

ONE OF THE MOST perplexing problems for any offense is preparing for a multiple defensive scheme. Trying to design an attack that will be effective against a myriad of defenses can drive a coach mad. It is just as disconcerting for the offensive players who must recognize each look and immediately make the needed blocking adjustments. You might then ask why everyone uses a multiple defensive scheme if it creates so much confusion. Below are some suggestions.

Strengths of Multiple Defenses

1. It places pressure on the blockers to recognize their assignment.
2. It increases the chances for a missed blocking assignment.
3. It can match a defensive strength against the biggest weakness of each style of offense.

Weaknesses of Multiple Defenses

1. It is hard to teach due to the multiplicity of techniques.
2. The individual techniques of each player are not refined.
3. Alignment errors are more frequent.
4. The risk of overcoaching is present with so many defenses.

Attacking Strategy

1. Call plays on the line of scrimmage after you see the defense.
2. Isolate the defensive tackle and run inside or outside depending on his alignment.
3. Run away from an overshifted free safety.

4. Show many formations in the hope of creating alignment errors in the secondary.

5. Run quick-hitting plays.

If a team uses a multiple defense package, they will usually possess an involved method of communication. It will require a formal huddle before each play. Most multiple defenses use a messenger system to get the change onto the field. Operate your offense without the use of a huddle. By elimination of your huddle, the defense is denied the use of the messenger and the opportunity to huddle as well. If they do want to change their defense, they have only one choice: to call the defense while the offense listens. When the opponent is denied the messenger, they end up playing one defense for several plays. This gives the advantage to the offense, since the opponent has built his hopes on creating confusion at the expense of defensive technique. By denying them the opportunity to change defenses as freely, the opponents are required to play technique football.

In many respects, the offense and defense have the same advantages and disadvantages when you play without a huddle. However, only the offense knows when these instances will occur; this permits you to determine the flow of the game. The defense can only respond; they are in no position to dictate the game's tempo. The shock value has a tremendous effect on the defense's mental poise the first time the offense aligns without a huddle. They are usually taken by such surprise that they will waste two of their time-outs in the first series of downs. If you are able to force the opponent into his base defense by eliminating the huddle, it should be fairly easy to pick his defense apart. Your plays can be flashed in from the sideline or the quarterback can call them at the line of scrimmage if he is mature enough to understand the game plan. The latter method is seldom used without a crib sheet attached to the quarterback's arm or center's rump.

If one of your opponents rotates through seven different defenses during the course of the game, it creates play selection problems. The nose guard would align in a different position on each of the defenses. This makes it easy for your quarterback to call the right play. Draw a grid on the rump of the center's pants, and list the best play to run against each defense in the square that corresponds to his alignment. The quarterback would check the location of the designated opponent, look down on the center's rump, and find the play written in the corresponding square. Flip-flop the offensive strength to mix-up the attack, even if you are running the same play most of the time.

Running Inside or Outside

Most of the time it is not easy to detect the various defenses, so we have devised a standardized plan for making the proper play selection. Our signal caller had to have an easy method of selecting the proper area and play, so we came up with a plan that would focus on an individual defender and not on the whole defense. Then we permitted everyone on the offense to help the quarterback with the call.

When the offense is over the ball, the quarterback will locate the free safety (number 6) by counting from the strong side to the weak side. (See Diagram 9–1.) Using the rules set in Chapter 4, the quarterback will announce the side he plans to attack. At this point the linemen will decide the play. First, the end locates the man with deep third responsibility. In Diagram 9–1, it is number 5 to the strong side and number 6 to the weak side. Once he has located deep third responsibility, your focus can be placed on number 3, the man to be optioned (in this case the defensive end). The tight end or slot will call number 3's position in relation to himself, i.e., inside or outside. If he is over the slot, the call will be made according to the type of charge he expects. If number 3 is aligned inside your slotback he will tell everyone you are running the option, as shown in Diagram 9–2.

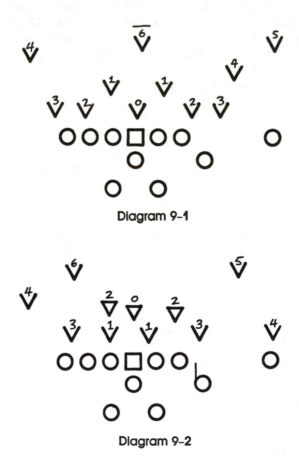

Diagram 9–1

Diagram 9–2

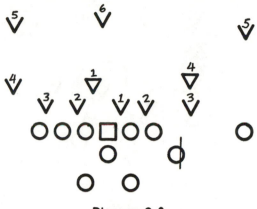

Diagram 9-3

If number 3 is aligned outside the slot or tight end, progress to the second step of your play-selection process as shown in Diagram 9-3. This call is made by the onside guard. He will spot the location of the first lineman beyond the center. If he is aligned head on or in the guard's outside gap, a call is made designating this. If he is aligned in the inside gap, another call is made. When this defender is over or outside, the call will be the rule-blocked dive. If number 1 is aligned in the inside gap, the rule-blocked outside veer is called.

To further diversify the attack, use the unbalanced formation when the situation warrants. There are several advantages to using the unbalanced approach against multiple defenses. Foremost is the problem it presents the defense in multiplicity of alignment. Not only must they know all their alignments and responsibilities for the various defenses they use, but when they face the unbalanced set they must learn the proper adjustments in each defense. This greatly increases chances for an adjustment error. Opponents who are wary of this problem prepare a standard adjustment to the unbalanced look and negate the object of their multiple scheme. You don't have the same problem, since you are keying in on individual alignments within each defense. Your chances of exploiting any alignment error have greatly increased without the danger of confusing your blockers.

When you align in the unbalanced set, the flipped-over guard will call the defense's adjustment to the offensive shift. He will count the third man out from the center and check to see if this is the same player the slotback is pointing to as the third man in from the player responsible for the deep third. Diagram 9-4 shows a defense where the third man out from the center and the third man in from deep third are the same player. In this instance it is obvious that you should attack to the long side, since the defense is outflanked. In Diagram 9-5, the defense has adjusted a full man to the unbalanced formation.

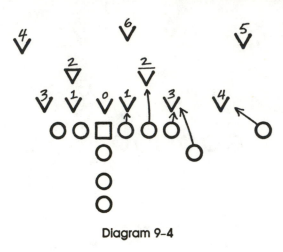

Diagram 9-4

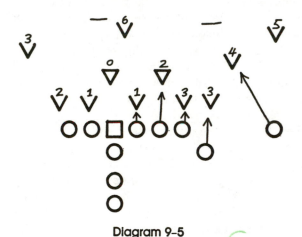

Diagram 9-5

Now there are two defenders designated as number 3 by the count of the flipped-over guard and the slotback. This alerts the guard to call a weakside counter, since it is obvious the defense is weak to the short side. Depending on the game plan and the opponent's defensive philosophy, run the quick trap, wingback scissors, or counteroption to the shortside. The choice of the weakside play should be made long before the game to prevent any confusion at the line of scrimmage. This gives you a complete running game against the multiple defense without ever needing to huddle. You can run the option, dive, outside veer, left, or right from balanced or unbalanced look, or counter from unbalanced. The quarterback need only decide which way you are going: then the guards, tackles, and slotback will make the rest of the decisions for him. You will be very successful using color calls to verbalize the signals to the quarterback. You can call a play in five seconds by using live and dead colors, leaving the defense completely in the dark.

Here is a brief review of the order of the calls made at the line:

1. The quarterback designates the hot side (where you will run).

2a. The slotback or tight end designates the number 3, determining if you will run the option.

2b. If you are unbalanced, the flopped-over guard will determine if a counter is needed if the slotback has not called an option.

3. The inside guard will call an outside veer or dive with rule-blocking if the former callers have not made a call.

The offside will make dummy color calls at the same time to prevent the defense from determining your direction. This formula will work against any defense, whether balanced or unbalanced. If it seems too simplistic, it is because you don't want to confuse your people. Your goal is to neutralize the defense's multiplicity and confuse them by forcing them into frequent adjustments when you show your multiple offensive sets.

If the previous strategy seems too complex, you can successfully use a simpler method of play calling. This is referred to as the inside-outside theory. It is usually run in conjunction with the huddle when you can't afford to be outguessed on the must-downs. In the huddle, call either dive in or dive out. At the line of scrimmage, check the alignment of the number 2 defender to determine which play you will run. If number 2 is aligned outside the offensive tackle, the inside dive will be run. If he is playing an inside control technique, then the outside dive will be used.

If the quarterback and diveback are outstanding athletes, this inside-outside approach can be read by these players just as it is by the triple-option teams. This technique is especially good against teams that use the late shift as a surprise tactic. The offensive tackle will block number 2 anyway he can, while the diveback and quarterback read his block. The guard knows he is responsible for a number 1 LB. If he gets an inside call from the tackle, it is fairly certain the linebacker will be flowing quickly to the outside. It is his responsibility to fold around the tackle, if necessary, to beat the backer to the point of attack. The diveback aims directly at the inside hip of his tackle and will alter his route depending on the location of his blocker's helmet. If the head goes inside the defender, so does the back. If the head goes outside, the diveback will run the outside dive just inside number 3, who is being blocked by your slotback or tight end (see Diagram 9–6).

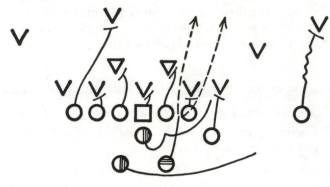

Diagram 9-6

Countering

When attacking the multiple defense in a conventional manner, certain counters are most effective. The key to successful counters is in giving the linemen enough time to determine their blocking method; if you rush them at the line, they may not have time to determine the proper blocking scheme. The blocking methods used are determined by the alignment of each defense. These blocking methods have been described in the preceding chapters. Slow-developing counters are not very effective against the multiple defense. The time they take to develop, combined with the chance of a missed blocking assignment, makes them high-risk choices. The quick-hitting fullback traps are the most effective counters.

10

How to Attack
Goal-Line Defenses
with the Run and Pass

IT HAS OFTEN been pointed out that the real test of an offense is its ability to score at the goal line. Many offenses do the job between the 10 yard lines, but falter just before attaining paydirt.

This offense has certainly proven its merit when knocking at the opponent's door.

Strengths of Goal-Line Defenses

1. Goal-line defense usually presents quick pressure in the gaps.
2. The close proximity of the defensive backs provides fast secondary pursuit.
3. The alignment and the philosophy of the defense affords all eleven defenders to be in the force unit.
4. The pass defense is aided by limited field depth.

Weaknesses of Goal-Line Defenses

1. Penetrating linemen can be trapped by quick offensive linemen.
2. Ballcarrier can be over-the-top versus low-charging defensive linemen.
3. Play-action passes can leave the maximum-run support defense vulnerable.
4. Pass receivers need only contact with two pass coverages (five short zone or man).

Attacking Strategy

1. Run quick traps vs. penetrating linemen.
2. Use play-action passes to get behind secondary coming in run support.

3. Run halfback option passes to threaten secondary dual responsibilities.

4. Run option with arc release to force perimeter into dual responsibilities.

5. Pass with crossing patterns to confuse man coverage secondary.

Running Outside

The base of the offense, the option, is certainly a big play versus the goal-line defenses. Generally, we prefer to run the option to the strongside versus the four deep looks and the weakside against the three deep defenses on the goal line. The guard pull gives the better seal blocks from the outside in, but it also allows the closely aligned secondary a head start in playing the run because of the key. See Diagram 10–1. Arc-block when running the option on the goal line, as shown in Diagrams 10–2 and 10–3. The onside tackle can usually hook-block the most dangerous defender, the defensive tackle opposite him, because he will be overly conscious of helping to stop the dive fake of the fullback.

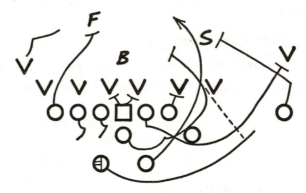

Diagram 10–1

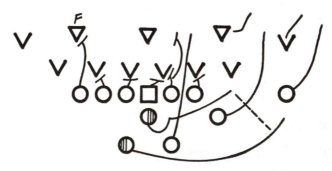

Diagram 10–2

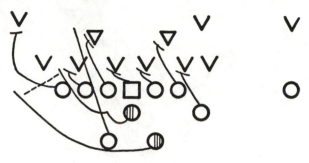

Diagram 10-3

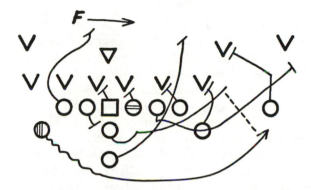

Diagram 10-4

The other defender who can cause trouble on the goal line is the strong guard; he penetrates the center's onside gap with such power that the center cannot control him. To solve this problem, run the option from the unbalanced line, permitting the onside tackle to angle-block him. If the defense does not move their front to the unbalanced, they will be out-flanked in this short yardage situation.

An opponent may not adjust to the unbalanced and still blow across so hard that he could stop the play before it gets started. In this instance use the unbalanced formation that puts the shifting guard next to the center, instead of outside the strongside tackle. This gives the offense the angle-block on both the guard and tackle. See Diagram 10-4.

Running Inside

When the goal-line defense has an open gap like the one usually presented by the sixty-five, attack the open gap. The lead-dive play has been most effective. The power I formation allows the power halfback a fast opportunity to get at the linebacker responsible for filling the open gap

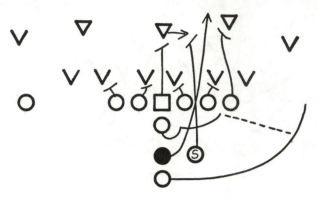

Diagram 10-5

(see Diagram 10-5). If the formation causes the defense to cheat the linebacker toward the open gap near the power halfback, the double dive from the splitback is a highly successful alternative, especially against the sixty-five. By diving both halfbacks in opposite directions, you will slow the middle linebacker's pursuit just enough to allow your slotback time to come through the open gap virtually unnoticed by the unsuspecting linebacker. This results in an outside-in trap-block. These same two approaches can be used against the wide tackle sixty-two look also. Run this play until the defense adjusts. Should the middle linebacker cheat toward the slot side of the formation, the straight dive to the tight end should strike fast enough to get the diveback into the hole before the backer can get there, especially if he has to beat the block of the center (see Diagram 10-6).

When the sixty-two guard squeezes the center, it is reasonably easy for him to block this technique. This frees the onside guard to block the inside linebacker while the onside tackle and slotback block defenders number 3 and number 4 respectively. The diveback angles his dive slightly wider to avoid an arm tackle from the guard. A note of caution: This blocking scheme can only be used occasionally (Diagram 10-7). If used as a steady diet on the goal line, the guard will alter his charge.

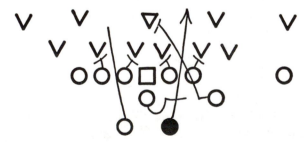

Diagram 10-6

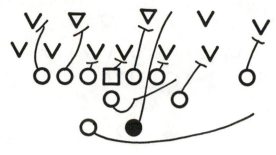

Diagram 10-7

Running Off-Tackle

When a defense can adjust to stop both the inside and outside plays, the goal-line offense boils down to the off-tackle game. The outside veer is the key play. Most defensive coaches hate to defend this play, especially inside their own 10 yard line, because of the shortage of people to defend all the choices. If your quarterback can read this play, it is virtually impossible to stop. The read should be easier in short yardage situations since the defense cannot afford to use cat-and-mouse techniques. The read is usually a quarterback keep as the number 3 man usually bites quick and hard to stop the threat of the wide diveback, who is the first threat to score. The block of the onside tackle is vital. If he can single-block the defensive number 2, you have the luxury of the slot blocking number 3 and the quarterback reading number 4 (see Diagram 10–8).

Versus the sixty-three, the trap-block is strong if the center has the ability to reach-block defender number 1 (see Diagram 10–9).

Use the arc-block with the outside veer to eliminate strong safety support on the diveback. Again, the onside tackle must be able to reach-block the tackle if you don't have the advantage of a down block (see Diagram 10–10).

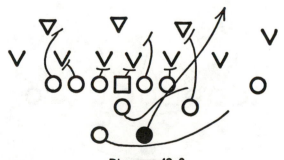

Diagram 10-8

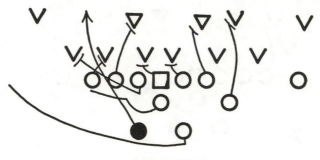

Diagram 10-9

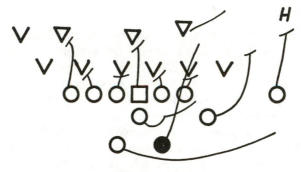

Diagram 10-10

Countering

The quick fullback trap is run one hole wider if the defensive number 1 gap technique is too strong to trap (see Diagram 10–11). If the number 1 defender aligns wider, the trap will be run with normal trap-blockings. It is also good when the inside linebackers in the split sixty-two flow quickly (Diagram 10–12). The scissors is not a play to use against goal-line defenses, although it can be worthwhile when an opponent reverts to a normal defense. This might occur near the 10 yard line in a third and long situation.

Diagram 10-11

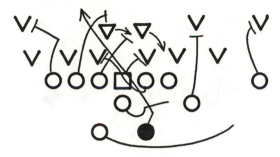

Diagram 10-12

PASSING ON THE GOAL LINE

The play-action style of passing gives you a tremendous weapon at the goal line, despite the limited depth the receivers have to operate. Your best pattern is a read-option slant or slant corner. This provides your split end with an excellent advantage in his one-on-one battle with the defensive back. The split end reads the alignment of the defensive back. If he is aligned to take away the outside, the slant is the call. If he is aligned to stop the slant, the slant corner is called. The split end signals the quarterback accordingly, gets the return signal and runs the prearranged route. The quarterback uses a two-step drop before he fires the ball on the slant. If the slant corner is pattern, the quarterback pump fakes the slant, fades two steps deeper and lofts a soft pass at the pylon in the corner of the end zone. The flexibility of this play makes it an excellent goal-line tool. (See Diagrams 10–13 and 10–14). A word of caution: Both of these pattern options are difficult and require a great deal of practice to perfect.

The second consideration, especially against the sixty-five defense, is the arc pass. The slotback runs the arc as described earlier and the quarterback reads the strong safety. If the strong safety covers the slotback on his pattern, the quarterback executes the option play. If the strong safety

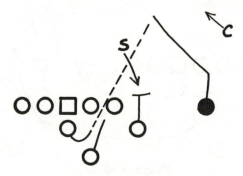

Diagram 10-13

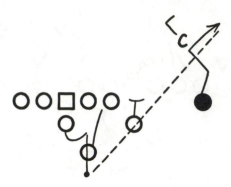

Diagram 10-14

defends the option play, the quarterback passes to the open slotback. However, the choice on this play does not end here. Often on the goal line the strong safety will try to perform the dual task of covering the slotback and then sprinting to cover the pitchback after the quarterback has read option. Once the quarterback is attacked and pitches to the running back, the running back assumes a run-or-pass role.

If he can reach paydirt on his own, he should immediately turn on the burners and streak for the end zone. If he sees scoring is not possible, he has three receivers spread out in front of him as shown in Diagram 10-15. The slotback, upon realizing the arc pass is not coming, turns to the outside, providing the running back with his first passing option. The split end, after his release, works to the corner of the end zone to be the second receiving possibility, and the quarterback, after executing the pitch, slips out in the flat as a third target.

The next consideration uses some aspects of the first two patterns. The split end releases as on a slant, but cuts his route almost parallel to the line of scrimmage. In the meantime the slot releases, using a modified arc,

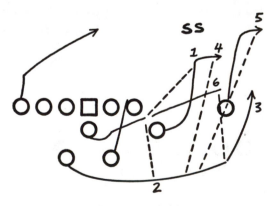

Diagram 10-15

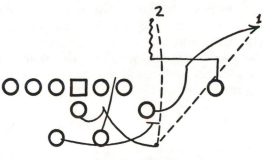

Diagram 10-16

and cuts to the outside under the split end, using him as a screen. The slotback is the primary target. If the defensive backs switch assignments and thereby eliminate the slotback as an open receiver, the split end will often be wide open just by drifting back toward the end line (see Diagram 10-16).

The slotback can also become a wide-open target when he slides behind your side of the scrimmage line just after a dive fake and block of the fullback. The pitch fake and block by your halfback also add to the deception. The slotback breaks through the line of scrimmage at the first opening from the center to the tight-end side, then breaks to the backside flat. The tight end releases inside and cuts across the middle at a depth of approximately five yards, clearing the area for the slotback as shown in Diagram 10-17. The quarterback in the meantime fakes to the diveback, then drops back. He waits for the slot to break open and passes for the wide open score.

Attack the tight-end side against the six-two defense: The pass is part of the package. The tight end becomes part of the scheme via the tight-end delay pass. This play is an excellent compliment to the outside veer at the tight end side. The faking fullback fill-blocks at the point of attack on number 3. The pitchback fakes the option and blocks the contain (number

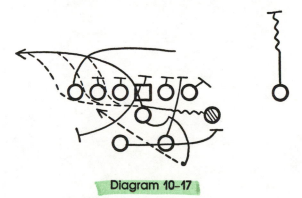

Diagram 10-17

4). The tight end blocks down for two counts to encourage the defense to read-run before he releases into the flat. The fake block release usually brings the defensive halfback to the line of scrimmage, permitting the tight end to slip into the corner wide-open. The quarterback must execute a good fake to the fullback before he pulls up and passes to the tight end for the score. See Diagram 10–18.

Diagram 10–18

11

How to Handle
the Special Situations

DURING THE COURSE of any football game, situations arise that can be classified as abnormal, and there are days that present abnormal playing conditions. This chapter is dedicated to these situations.

FIRST PLAY SPECIALS

There are times when you would like to set the tempo for the game by scoring on your first play from scrimmage. Opening the game with a trick play may get a quick score, but the strategy could backfire before the day is over. What will be the long-term effect of that play on the outcome of the game? Will it fire up your team and lead you to victory, or will it ignite a lethargic opponent and cause them to fight harder?

You should be able to gauge the long-term attitude of your team, but you can only speculate on the long-range attitude of your opponent. If your team has entered the game with a fanatical desire for victory, anything you do is in the best interest of your team. But this is not always the case. There are days when *your* team is lethargic, overconfident, or downright indifferent; likewise, your opponent may be just as dedicated to victory as you are. You must weigh all of these factors before you try the play. Ask yourself which combination of circumstances exists, and if it would be to your advantage to use a trick play in an effort to get on the scoreboard first.

If you feel your opponent can be shaken by a surprise move on your part, then by all means use the trick play to score first. If a quick score will arouse a sleeping giant it may be in your best interest to keep the giant snoozing, then spring the trick play when it will be too late for him to rise up and crush your upset bid

Assuming you feel the tide of battle can be turned in your direction with some early chicanery, here are a few specials that have proven successful over the years.

The Substitution Pitchout

On the play following the first kick return of the game, your team will explode with a quick score. Whether the opponent punts or kicks-off to you is not important. What the return team wants to do is return the kick toward the opponent's bench. When the officials mark the ball ready for play, it will be on the hash mark farthest from the offense's bench. The kick teams will leave the field and the opponent's defense will come onto the field and align or huddle near the football. In the meantime, the return team's units will be running at least 35 yards beyond the spot where the ball is set for the play. The offensive unit must travel 35 yards before they are in front of the waiting defense. The rules of play state that all players must be within 15 yards of the ball prior to the snap and that every player must be set for one second. If there are seven men facing downfield on the line of scrimmage within that 15 yard limit, it is permissible to start play.

The idea is for the team coming onto the field to set up quickly on the line of scrimmage with the widest man 2 yards inside the hash mark. The three backs can be anyplace inside that mark as long as they are stationary at the snap. The player that snaps the ball can be the original ballcarrier, the center, or a player sitting on the ground tying a shoelace. Whoever you select should be waiting casually at the hash mark for the officials to spot the ball. If the play is orchestrated properly, the ball will be snapped to a waiting back before the defenders can gain leverage on the offensive unit. When the decoy snaps the ball to the closest back, all the other players will set a wall just as they do on a punt return, while the two remaining backs act as lead blockers (see Diagram 11-1). Obviously you cannot use this play every Saturday, but it will come in handy when you *must* have a quick score that can mean the difference between a close defeat and a narrow victory.

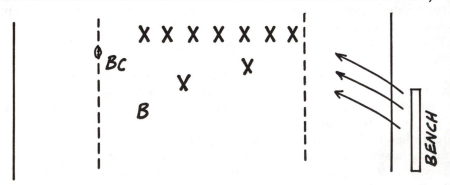

Diagram 11-1

Hash-Mark Huddle

This play is similar to the previous special but can be run at anytime during the game. From the start of the game the offense, with the exception of the center who aligns on the ball, will huddle near the line of scrimmage on the hash mark closest to their own bench. After the huddle the team runs over to the ball and sets up to run the play called in the huddle. In most cases the defense will move with the offense to be in a position of leverage on the unusual huddle, provided the center is near the ball. When the defenders stop following the huddle around the field and begin to align on the ball, you pull off the surprise quick snap to a back that breaks from the previous special. To make the play legal, the seven linemen must be facing downfield and all eleven players must be stationary for one second before the snap (see Diagram 11-2).

Both of these plays should be thoroughly explained to the officials prior to the game. You don't want them taken by surprise; it could result in an indiscriminate flag or aligning in a position that would impede the progress of the trick play.

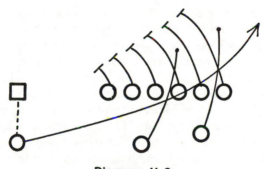

Diagram 11-2

Halfback Pass

The halfback pass is not a dramatic play, but it can be used as a surprise element in any football game. This play is standard fare for every option team. The key to its success is when it is unveiled. In a big game, when the tension is great, this play can be devastating.

At the start of the game the defensive halfback is anxious to get into the action. He has been coached all week to recognize the option: He sees it develop and comes up too fast. Later in the game when he is more relaxed, the play may not be as effective. By springing this play at the start of the game, it can take the wind out of the sails of many aggressive defensive backs. We use the basic option blocking on this play, except we call "pass" in the huddle to alert our blockers not to go downfield. The split end will

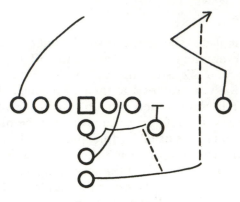

Diagram 11-3

maneuver just as he does on the option, until he is about 6 yards downfield. At this point he breaks hard to the flag and looks for the ball over his outside shoulder (see Diagram 11-3).

Reverse Pass

At the start of every game, the players on both teams are usually anxious for the action and will respond quickly to a trick play. Because of this, the end-around pass has a very good chance of success. The secondary is fresh and alert and will quickly recognize the split-end reverse. The far halfback will come up to support, permitting the tight end to slip beyond him. The slotback or fullback is also brought underneath, just in case the halfback is not fooled. The line blocks the play the same as they do on the bootleg pass (mentioned in Chapter 1). The quarterback will pitch past the running back directly to the end (see Diagram 11-4). This play is even more effective if the split-end reverse has been used in recent weeks. The defenders will react more quickly to the reverse action if it is in their scouting report.

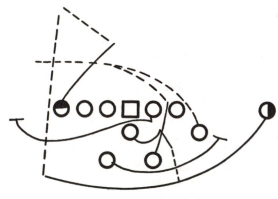

Diagram 11-4

WASTE-DOWN SPECIALS

A waste down is usually classified as second and one in the three-down zones, or third and one in the four-down zones. Since the offense should be able to make the needed yardage for the first down on the following play, this down can be wasted if you want to try for the big play. The waste-down play can be simply the long play-action pass or a more elaborate series of plays. Pattern these plays after the antics of a magician. The magician explains what he is going to do, and you watch closely to figure out how he does the trick. Knowing this, he shows you a lot of meaningless action to distract you from his real intentions. On waste-down plays the opponent knows you are in a position to go for a quick score and will usually set their defense to give you the first down, but they will loosen the secondary to prevent you from taking advantage of them deep. To counter this strategy, show them a play that they will recognize, then produce something new from that action.

In Chapter 3 there are a number of deep play-action passes that you could use in waste-down situations. When used properly, these can become good all-or-nothing selections. The belly option halfback pass already shown in Diagram 11–3 is always a possibility in these situations, as is the fake counteroption shown in Diagram 6–13.

THIRD AND RIDICULOUS

This is when you don't want to call the play. Usually a 15-yard penalty and a lost-yardage play have backed you up so far that there is little hope of making a first down. Because of your poor position, the opposing team will loosen their perimeter to prevent you from climbing out of the hole.

In most cases a high-consistency play is the best choice to escape from this predicament. The dive or option can break big because the defense is spread out over a larger than normal area. Of these two choices the dive will usually get more yardage than the option since the perimeter people are in good position to keep leverage on wide plays.

To pass, you will be given the very short passes under the linebackers or the short hooks in seams of the zones. The looseness of the defense provides an opportunity to get back that lost yardage. Since they will give up the inside run or short pass, you have the potential of breaking a big gain with a lateral following the short completion. It is not the ingenuity of the play that will provide the big gain, but the surprise factor of the lateral. The defense is counting on good pursuit angles to keep all gains to a minimum. They will be coming hard from all directions once the pass is completed. The well-timed lateral could easily break the contain and get back the needed yardage. Diagrams 11–5 and 11–6 show two successful flea-flicker passes.

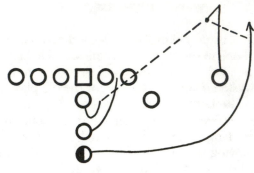

Diagram 11-5

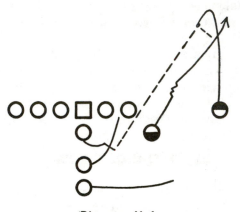

Diagram 11-6

In Diagram 11-5, the split end will take advantage of the loose secondary by running a three-step stop pattern. The running back will sprint toward the sideline on the snap, working on as much width as possible before turning upfield. All the secondary pursuit will be aimed at the wide receiver. If this play fails it is because the lateral comes too quickly; there must be a slight delay between the catch and the lateral. The receiver must hold onto the ball for a couple of seconds to permit the defender enough time to establish uncontrolled angles of pursuit on him. By pitching it too soon they will merely adjust courses that have not yet developed and make the tackle for no gain.

In Diagram 11-6, the lateral is made deeper at the end of a curl route by the split end. This type of flea-flicker is effective when the linebackers are tight and the secondary is loose. The receiver will curl up in the seam between the zones while he waits for the slotback to sprint underneath him on an upfield angle. The slotback should release off the line of scrimmage slowly and should not accelerate until he sees the ball is on the way to the split end. If this lateral can be made, the play could achieve much more success than just gaining a first down because the slotback will be beyond the last line of defense if the lateral can be properly timed.

FOURTH AND SHORT

In this situation, everyone usually knows what play is coming. You give the ball to your best back on your best play and run behind your best linemen. But there are times when you feel a first down probably won't lead to a score, so you can take advantage of the certainty of the situation and gamble with the big play. Diagram 11-7 shows an example of this thinking. If your best short-yardage play is the lead dive, a seam pass-off that has backfield action is very effective.

Both the quarterback and split end must take their time for this play to be successful. The quarterback must hang tough on the ride with the fullback to draw the linebackers into the dive hole, and the split end must feign a block on the cornerback to draw him close. When he closes, your end breaks to the inside and the quarterback disengages from the fullback and lofts a soft pass to him. The timing of the end's separation from the cornerback and the subsequent removal of the ball from the fullback's belly are critical. If the quarterback pulls the ball before the split end separates, the play is dead. If the quarterback waits too long to pass the ball, the play will fail also because the defensive back will recover his lost cushion.

When you want to maintain possession but don't want to take a risk, the safest maneuver is to draw the opponent offsides. The easiest way to do this is to snap the ball on the long count; this is especially effective if you always snap the ball on the same count. Drawing your team offsides is the

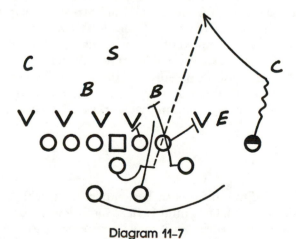

Diagram 11-7

obvious danger. This can be remedied by not giving the team a play; since they have no assignment, they cannot jump offsides. If the defense will not be drawn offsides, the quarterback can pause and call the play at the line of scrimmage. If the offense only does this once or twice a game, the defense will not be able to determine the point of attack.

INCLEMENT WEATHER

Since you play football in all types of weather and on all sorts of playing surfaces, a plan is needed to deal with rain, mud, and wind. Each of these conditions presents a different problem for the offense and will be treated separately.

1. Rain

The ball becomes the biggest problem on a rainy day, especially if the quarterback has small hands. The field may not be as much an issue as the ball. The ability to control the ball usually deteriorates as the game progresses, so scoring early is of primary importance. First you want to eliminate as much ball handling as possible. This means that the fullback ride, especially on the outside-veer play, becomes very risky. It is hard for the quarterback to seat the slippery ball and even harder for the fullback to gain control of it.

The option play is not as dangerous in the rain. The ball can be tossed softly and slowly, giving the pitchback time to look the ball in, while a handoff can be clumsy. Since long drives are not the order of the day in the rain, play-action passes are more important on first or second down early in the game. If you have special passes designed for a particular opponent on this type of day, save them for the second half. Stress the play-action passes immediately to gain the early score. If you don't connect on the big play, you can punt and let the opponent worry about handling the slick ball.

If you enter the season with a quarterback that has small hands, a power off-tackle play will be needed in the offensive repertoire. If he cannot handle a wet ball, the secondary is going to be standing on the line of scrimmage, and there is no option that works well against an eleven-man front.

2. Mud

There is a definite difference between playing with a wet ball and playing on a sloppy field. On a muddy field footing is the problem, not ball handling. If the grass is worn out it may be impossible to run an option in the center of the field. The defense that backs off the ball will gain a definite advantage while defending against the quarterback that seems to be moving in slow motion toward the corner. In these instances the option develops so slow that it can be effectively pursued and run out of bounds. If there is grass beyond the hash marks, you must run the option into the short side of the field to get sufficient footing. Counters and reverses are the best outside plays on muddy fields because the ballcarrier will not have to make a cut to make the counter work. It is the defender who must change direction to stop a properly executed counter. This is a definite advantage for the offense.

Knowing that long-scoring drives are out of the question, play-action passes should become an early down staple, just as on rainy days. Since the quarterback will have problems with his footwork, it may be worthwhile to consider including a shotgun formation in the offensive notebook. (In Chapter 15 the potential of the shotgun in the belly option attack is discussed.) The quarterback starting 5 yards off the line of scrimmage does not have to be concerned with pivoting and changing direction, nor with the worries involved in setting up to pass.

3. *Wind*

Running the offense on windy days requires more common sense than strategy. Everyone wants to run the ball into the wind and pass when the wind is at their backs.

When the wind is in your face and passing becomes a very dangerous strategy, it is vital to speed up the clock. This means that you cannot run out of bounds or call timeouts. You should take as much time as you can in the huddle and be as slow as possible when unpiling after each play. The running game should consist of high-consistency plays. Your main objective is to get first downs and control the ball.

When the wind is behind you, use the low-consistency plays. These plays have the potential to break the game open. Even if you fail to make a big play, an average wind-aided punt will get your defense excellent field position. This does not mean that you should throw a lot of long passes. On the contrary, long passes with the wind are just as inaccurate as passes into the wind. The passing game must be kept short because the wind will carry the ball beyond the receiver's reach. It is just too difficult for the quarterback to control a ball thrown long in any direction when the wind is blowing hard.

LAST POSSESSION OF THE FIRST HALF

This is not a desperation situation but one which can be used to set the tempo for the second half. Since time is a factor, you will not be able to engineer a long drive. But it would be foolish to waste a possession. A quick score before the half is always good for team morale, but if that cannot be achieved you should at least send the opponent into the locker room with a new problem. This leaves you with two choices: either run some sort of a special play that may get a quick score or introduce some unusual offensive concept into the game that can dominate the opponent's half-time meeting. The more time they spend discussing your gimmick, the less time they will spend talking about game strategy.

Statue of Liberty

Knowing the defense expects a long pass, you show regular belly option play action, sending the tight end on a deep-post move. The running back will turn around in the same manner the split end does on the reverse pass. The quarterback will simply hand him the ball as he goes by. The line blocking is the same as it is on the split end reverse pass, except the uncovered linemen will release to the downfield running lane after a three-count delay (see Diagram 11–8).

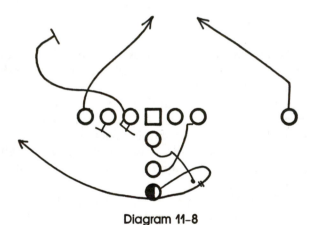

Diagram 11-8

Statue Pass

This pass uses the same blocking scheme as the previous reverse pass. It is designed to be run later in the same game as the aforementioned Statue of Liberty play. As you can see in Diagram 11–9, the tight end releases deep into the area covered by the free safety. The split end should sprint across the field just beyond the linebackers and break toward the far flag as the far corner rotates up to stop the statue run threat. The running back will locate the free safety and pass opposite him to either the tight end or slotback. The open receiver should be behind the opposing secondary. If he has not slipped behind everyone, the back should not attempt the pass.

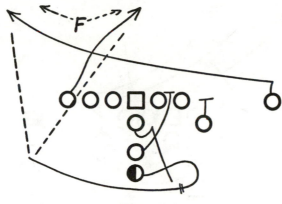

Diagram 11-9

Fake-Statue Pass

This is the third pass of this particular special. This time the quarter-back will go through all the motions of running the Statue of Liberty to the running back, and, after a brief pause, will pass to the tight end dragging through the deep secondary. The key to this play is the acting job the quarterback does on the fake statue. When the back passes behind him the quarterback pivots so his back is turned away from the line of scrimmage and his eyes follow the runningback. In the meantime, he rests the ball on the hip farthest from the near defensive end. For a moment he will be totally unprotected. His body langauge must tell the pass rushers and free safety that the running back has taken the ball. After a brief pause, he presents the ball again and passes to the tight end as shown in Diagram 11-10. These are high-risk plays, but the players love them. By changing them every few weeks it helps keep the players' interest at a high level.

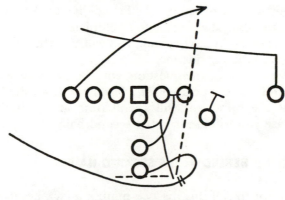

Diagram 11-10

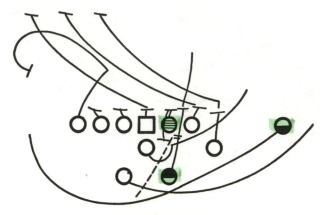

Diagram 11-11

Another successful trick play for this situation is shown in Diagram 11-11. It is a hidden-ball play that is as new as the single wing buck lateral. The quarterback gives the ball to the fullback just as he would on any dive; then he and the tailback continue the option fake. The uncovered lineman in front of the fullback will turn his back to the line of scrimmage after the play starts, while remaining in a crouched position. As the fullback passes him, he transfers the ball to the waiting lineman and continues downfield. The lineman will not rise up or move from the spot but wait for the split end to come across the backfield at a depth of about 8 yards. The end cannot arrive too quickly or the deception caused by the missing ball will not materialize.

As he passes behind the line, the ball is flipped back to him and the race to the corner is on. He usually needs one block to make the far corner. This is provided by the tight end who starts down just as he does on the option, then peels back behind the near halfback and gets into position to pick him off when the end makes the turn to pursue the split end. All the other players will block their count man toward the split side until they loose contact. Then they will sprint toward the far sideline to become a clean-up blocker. Usually the defense will come to a complete halt when they realize that none of the three backs has the ball. This will give the split end a slight edge on his sprint to the far sideline.

If a score seems out of the question, you should have some unusual formation prepared that can be used for a few plays. It should be threatening enough that the opponent will spend time at the half preparing adjustments in case you will use it in the second half.

BEHIND IN THE SECOND HALF

You don't want to call this the two-minute attack because it may be more than that. If you are behind in the second half, you must go into your hurry-up offense when there is still enough time left to catch up. For example, there are about eleven possessions in each high school game and there are approximately thirteen in each college game. You will have to abandon your game plan when you have the same number of possessions left as you are touchdowns behind. If you are three scores down, you must go into the hurry-up offense on the ninth possession in high school and on the eleventh in college.

Obviously, the hurry-up attack will not be effective if it is built around play-action passes because no one with a big lead is going to be fooled by them. You must come right out and do what they expect: throw the ball and run wide. The first objective is to slow down the clock; you must stop the clock after every play. This means your attack should include a straight sprint-out pass designed to get the ball out of bounds. This play should be known to every offensive player so it can be used at anytime without the need of a huddle. When you call "Hurry Up," everyone should automatically line up and run this particular play (see Diagram 11–12). Every time the clock is still running at the end of a play, the offense will line up in this formation and run this play.

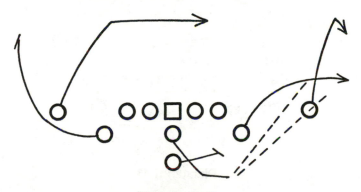

Diagram 11–12

You do not want to waste a down by throwing the ball out of bounds; you always want to move the ball upfield, even in this situation. When the clock is stopped, the offense can huddle and new plays can be sent in from the sideline. These should be low-consistency plays that are capable of eating up large chunks of ground. The only time to use a high-consistency play is when a first down is needed to keep possession of the ball. Never disregard the option as a potential weapon. It is very effective against prevent defenses, provided the quarterback pitches the ball and the running back gets out of bounds.

AHEAD LATE IN THE GAME

Use the same formula in the last half to determine when you are out of danger. When ahead by more scores than your opponent has potential possessions, you can substitute freely. As long as the game is in jeopardy, run only high-consistency plays while trying to stay in bounds. Try to use the clock in the way you would when running into the wind.

FINAL PLAY OF THE GAME

When the clock is almost gone and you are within a touchdown of victory, you must come up with one play capable of pulling the game out of the fire. Since the defense is going to be spread all the way back to their goal line, you have no chance of getting behind them; any scoring play must develop in front of the waiting secondary. Two plays will pull you out of the situation. They are rugby-type plays that develop off your basic split-end curl and tight-end hook as shown in Diagrams 11–13 and 11–14. These are flea-flickers that include an option following the first lateral. The loose zone coverage should enable you to complete the short 12 to 14 yard-pass to the end. The pursuit will close in on the player receiving the

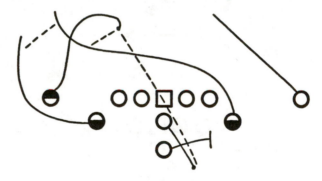

Diagram 11–13

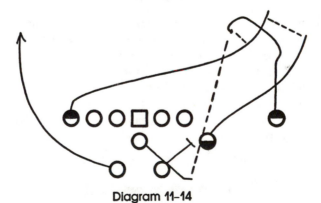

Diagram 11–14

lateral, allowing him to pitch the ball to a third receiver who is waiting along the sideline. For an option football team this type of ball handling should not be very difficult.

The other possibility is the bomb-and-tip play shown in Diagram 11–15. On this play three receivers will converge at a spot about 30 to 40 yards downfield, bringing with them several more defenders. The ball is thrown high into the pack and everyone will jump up in an attempt to deflect the ball. The offensive players will try to deflect the ball further upfield to the end coming from the opposite side of the field. Assuming all the defenders converge on the pass, the isolated receiver will have a chance to catch the deflection if it is tipped far enough from the pack. This is a very low-consistency play, but it has been completed—ask Franco Harris.

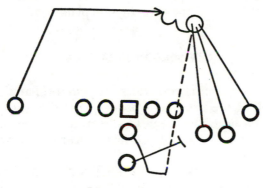

Diagram 11–15

Developing
an Effective Game Plan

WHEN YOU HAVE all of the weapons necessary for a successful offense, you must turn your attention to the actual game plan.

OFF-SEASON PLANNING

As a dedicated mentor, you will start your preparations in the off-season. Review all of the previous seasons' game films in detail. Evaluate the returning personnel of both teams to determine potential strengths and weaknesses. The personnel are of primary concern when you formulate a potential game plan.

Now that time is not a factor, do a fine-tooth-comb breakdown of each play. Parts of this procedure are actually started during the season. The day after the game, each play's efficiency is evaluated as part of the preparation for the next game. In the off-season this review is expanded beyond the simple efficiency rating and problem areas. Now you want to determine the how and why of the total offense by taking a careful look at your success against the defense on every play.

Use the Master Film Grading Form (see Diagram 12–1) which, as already mentioned, is started during the season; additional details are added to the form in the off-season. A written synopsis of each decision is recorded with each diagram when necessary. Every blocking scheme is also evaluated. Suggestions for improvement or changes in schemes are made. A major goal of the film review is to pinpoint the plays and blocking schemes that should be retained for that opponent next fall.

Also evaluate the opponent's techniques versus each play run in regard to blocking style, play, execution, etc.

Once the breakdowns are completed, turn your attention to the master book kept on every opponent. Complete records are kept on file in the large binder. An overhaul is performed on each opponent's book in the off-season. Material included but not necessarily limited to this list is as follows:

Put in Name, No., and Position						LT	LG	C	RG	RT	TE	SB	SE	QB	FB	TB
Play No.	Down	Dist.	Hash	Yd. Line	Play-Defense											

Diagram 12-1

135

1. *Complete Scouting Reports.* These reports are kept for a minimum of five years. If space becomes a problem, a written synopsis is made. After the five-year period they may be discarded. See Diagram 12–2 for an outline of the items included in a scouting report.

2. *Film Breakdowns.* Use the same five-year consideration. See Diagram 12–3 for a form of the film breakdown synopsis.

3. *Complete Game Reminders.* These include the total game plan and once again five years' worth is kept on file. See Diagram 12–4 for an outline of a game reminder.

4. *Post-Game Critique.* This too is another five-year item. These forms (see Diagram 12–5) are filled out the day after the game by the staff when everything is still fresh in everyone's mind. This item is an invaluable tool when planning for the next year.

5. *Master Tendency File.* This file has no time limit. It is a synopsis of all the defensive tendencies, adjustments, and areas of weakness you have gathered on the opponents. Over the years this file will show the innermost philosophies of each defense. It will also give you a quick source of information on something not shown prior to your game in a particular year.

Once the off-season film review and subsequent opponent review is completed, you are encouraged to develop a tentative game plan. Meet in the late spring to revise your offense for the coming fall, and take into consideration the thoughts each coach has for his tentative game plan. These plays will all be placed in the offensive manual.

Work on your game plan during the summer at your leisure. Then at the pre-season meeting review your total offense, including practice procedures and techniques. Compile a simplified game plan for each opponent.

SCOUT REPORT

Cover

Artwork and motivational material for opponent.

Overview

Scouts ratings of opponents various systems and what we must do to win. Tips for our various units regarding opponent.

Opponent's Offense

Depth

Regulars and substitutes at each position including: height, weight, class, jersey number, and comments.

Kicking

Complete look at their offensive kicking game including: diagram, personnel, etc.

Formations and Plays

Diagrams of all formations and most plays used.

Opponent's Defense

Depth

Same as under offense except for their defense.

Kicking

Same as under offense except for their defense.

Looks and Adjustments

Diagrams of most defensive alignments, adjustments, coverages, and stunts used.

Diagram 12-2

DEFENSIVE NOTES

What is their basic scheme against us?

How is this different from our scouting report?

Short yards defense?
Is it new? _____

Long yards defense?
Is it new? _____

What plays worked best
against them?   What did they stuff?

Formation	Play	Formation-Play	Reason
1.		1.	
2.		2.	
3.		3.	
4.		4.	
5.		5.	

Formation	Passes		
1.		1.	
2.		2.	
3.		3.	

Diagram 12–3

GAME REMINDERS

Cover
Artwork and motivational material for opponent.

Itinerary
Dress roster plus coaches, managers, trainers, and the like; coach's message; in-depth time schedule.

Game Organization
List of all units and substitutions plus bench or sideline organization.

Diagram 12–4

Defensive Reminders

Kicking

List of "do's" and "don'ts" for all phases of the defensive kicking game.

Game Plan

Complete game plan (calls, coverages, adjustments).

Line

List of "do's" and "don'ts" for the defensive line.

Linebackers

Same as for defensive line except for linebacker.

Backs

Same as for defensive line except for the secondary.

Offensive Reminders

Kicking

Same as defense except for our offense.

Game Plan

Complete game plan: general plus normal situations by position on field plus special situations (i.e., two minute, two-point plays).

Line

Same as for defensive line except for offensive line.

Receivers

Same as for defensive line except for receivers.

Backs

Same as for defensive line except for the secondary.

Diagram 12-4 (Continued)

POST-GAME CRITIQUE

Opponent and Year: _____

1. Where did they hurt us and why?

    A. List plays, defensive errors, unexpected offense, etc.

2. Where did they stop us and why?

    A. List adjustments, offensive mistakes, unexpected defense, etc.

3. Comment on all kicking game areas:
    > Punt
    > Punt Return
    > KO
    > KO Return
    > PAT/FG
    > PAT/FG Defense
    > Miscellaneous

4. Who were their best defensive, offensive, and kicking players? (Names, Numbers, Class, etc.)

    > **D =**

    > **O =**

    > **K =**

5. What were our best defensive schemes against them?

6. What were our best plays or blocking schemes against them?

7. Overall remarks about game for next year's file.

Diagram 12–5

IN-SEASON PLANNING

Once you get into the actual season, turn your attention from seasonal planning and generalized game plans to specific game strategies for the opponent of the week. Base your final decisions on two major factors: the opponent's scouting report and the exchange film of the opponent. The scouting report is extremely important to your game plan. You need to know all the opponent's defenses and adjustments. Try to predict each adjustment the opposition will use against your proposed formations. The value of the people scouting can be measured in touchdowns; depend on their scouting skills as you create the final game plan.

They must understand your philosophies and be able to recognize the opponent's potential reactions to your attacking methods; they are to record everything possible and then break it down by situation.

This portion of the scouting report is hard work. Completing all of the forms is tedious and time consuming. Fortunately for your programs, you can ease this task by using a new computer scouting program, which computes the various tendencies gathered for the down and distance, field position, and hash-mark charts. You can also get the results of each defensive call.

The computer also provides a quick means of compiling and sorting the opponent's various pass coverages. The scouts add any keys that may tip each of these coverages. The computer also categorizes the efficiency of each of the opposition's defensive calls. Once this report is printed, compare it to the previous year's scouting report and your previous year's game film breakdown versus the opponent. This enables you to answer the following questions:

1. Did they change from the previous report?
2. Do they have common defensive plans for us?
3. Does it change from year to year?
4. What worked best for us in the past?

The second component in your game plan is the film exchange. Although it does not provide you with an actual on-the-spot report, you will get much more information from it than your in-person scouting reports. By carefully analyzing the opponent's film you can generate all the information desired. Forms similar to scouting report charts are used to secure all of the needed data. You are also able to fill in the voids left by the scout. This is especially true in evaluating the various techniques used by your opponent's defensive personnel. This gives your offensive staff the opportunity to compare your blocking techniques with their charges; you can determine the ability of the opposing players.

The scouts break down the film just as they did when they scouted the opponent. This gives the scout at least two looks at each opponent. Have your scouts review last year's game of the team to be scouted before they actually go on the scouting assignment. This three-pronged approach gives the scouts a reasonably comprehensive knowledge of the opponent in question.

GAME WEEK PLANNING

The scouts compile all their data for presentation prior to the Sunday night staff meeting. They present the material orally and also provide the staff with a written report. Following the meeting, the exchange film is scrutinized by the scout with the offensive staff. The scout leads the staff through this review, attempting to give each coach a feel for the opponent. Once the film review is completed, the offensive staff prepares a rough game plan using your Game Planning Guide (see Diagram 12-6). This phase of your preparation will be time consuming and provocative but should be completed before the meeting is adjourned. On Monday the offensive coaches will continue to review the film with a fine-tooth comb. They will search for things that may have been missed that could give you additional insight into your opponent's defensive scheme.

At your Monday players' meeting, review your previous week's game film and attempt to use it as a teaching tool for the next game; then that game is laid to rest and all your efforts are geared toward the next opponent. Next the scouting film is reviewed by the entire offensive squad. At this meeting the staff alerts the players to each point they think is significant. Look to the opponent's defenses and adjustments as well as to their personnel. Then your attack is dissected so that each player gets a picture of his individual job and your total team approach. At the same time, your scouts should take the scout team to another area and familiarize them with the defenses they will be using during practice. Conclude the meeting by completely previewing next week's game plan. After the meeting your staff will try to finalize this game plan. But there will be times when you will have to make changes on Tuesday.

On Tuesday and Wednesday, expect each of your players to review the exchange film in detail. They should watch the man they are to block, noting how the player delivers a blow, how he steps, and if he plays high or low. Each of your players should then discuss with his position coach any tendencies or weaknesses he has found.

Incorporate anything your squad members pick up on the film because it makes everybody feel they are contributing to your game plan. Some of these points may be extremely valuable on game day.

On Tuesday, start to practice your game plan. Prior to practice, prepare a list with each play to be run and the defense to be used against that play. This is known as a script and when properly prepared it enables each coach to be a more efficient and effective teacher. The script prepares

GAME PLANNING GUIDE

Additional Formations, etc.

Pro, X Pro, Over, X Over, Flanker, X Flanker, Twins, Spread, Split, Tight, list others.

Running Plays and Blocking

Speed–Count, Wedge, Cross, Switch, Double, Lead, Fold, Cross and Lead, Sucker, list others.

Counter Speed–Count, Influence, Trap, Fold, Lead, Special Lead, list others.

Scissors–Count, Fold, Trap, Fold and Lead, list others.

Sneak–Count, Wedge, Tap and Go, list others.

Option–Count, G, Arc, G–Arc, Lead, list others.

Counter Option–Rule (Arc–off G), G, list others.

Passing Actions and Blocking Adjustments

Dream, Scissors, Option, Bootleg, Roll, list others.

Passing Patterns

Long–Post, Long, Out and Long, list others.

Medium–Out, In, Hook, Flood, list others.

Short–Stop, Scramble, Slant, Pitch, Arc, list others.

Goal Line—Short Yardage Offense

Runs–Speed, C Speed, Dream, Option, list others and blocking.

Passes–Pick, Corner, Flood, Bootleg, list others.

Situation

2 Minute, Fake Kick (List)   Audible, list others.
Specials

Diagram 12-6

everyone to do the optimum teaching job on each play. Group your plays by down and distance and by hash-mark and field position; this gives you simulated game conditions without being redundant. Diagram 12–7 shows a sample script. Following practice, each player is given a take-home test on all his blocking assignments against every defense they expect to face (see Diagram 12–8); each player is also expected to take a short scouting report test on the opponent's defense (see Diagram 12–9).

Wednesday is much like Tuesday, except for needed revisions in the game plan. Once again, the players are given another take home test on their assignments. Thursday is review day and the final game plan is rehearsed. The written scouting reports are turned in on Thursday after practice and Game Reminders are issued to the players dressing for the game. Each player is expected to spend time with his Reminder so he will be well-prepared by kick-off time.

Friday's plans will vary from year to year, but one drill will prove worthwhile every year. This is the preview of the game plan with the players dressed in shorts. In it, two different units will alternately attack one defensive squad.

The Game Plan Chart is used and the ball is moved around the field so every situation is covered. Substituting (an important consideration) is practiced, and all units are carefully prepped for order of use on Saturday. The Game Reminders are reviewed and a test is given after practice. As with the scouting test (see Diagram 12–10), each position coach checks the answers of the players in his area. A meeting is also held with the quarterbacks to review procedures and calls to be used in the game. On Saturday (or game day) the offensive staff goes through one final review. Each coach has a chart of everything he must cover to ensure that nothing is forgotten, and each position group will have a final review meeting before they leave for the game.

OFFENSIVE SEQUENCE

(Year)   (Opponent)

Goal Line (List formation, play, defense, and situation.)

1.   5.
2.   6.
3.   7.
4.   8.

L	M	R

Normal (List formation, play, defense, and situation.)

1.

2.

3.

4.

5.

Long

6.

7.

8.

Short

9.

10.

Two Minute Offense (Calls except Scramble)

1.   3.   5.

2.   4.   6.

Diagram 12–7

NAME_____ HOLE— { 1 2 6 MAN 8 9 5 4 GREEN
POSITION_____   SPRINT DRAW SCREEN

RULE:_____ CIRCLE THE ONE YOU ARE DOING
              RULE:_____ RULE:_____
HOLE#_____ HOLE#_____ HOLE#_____

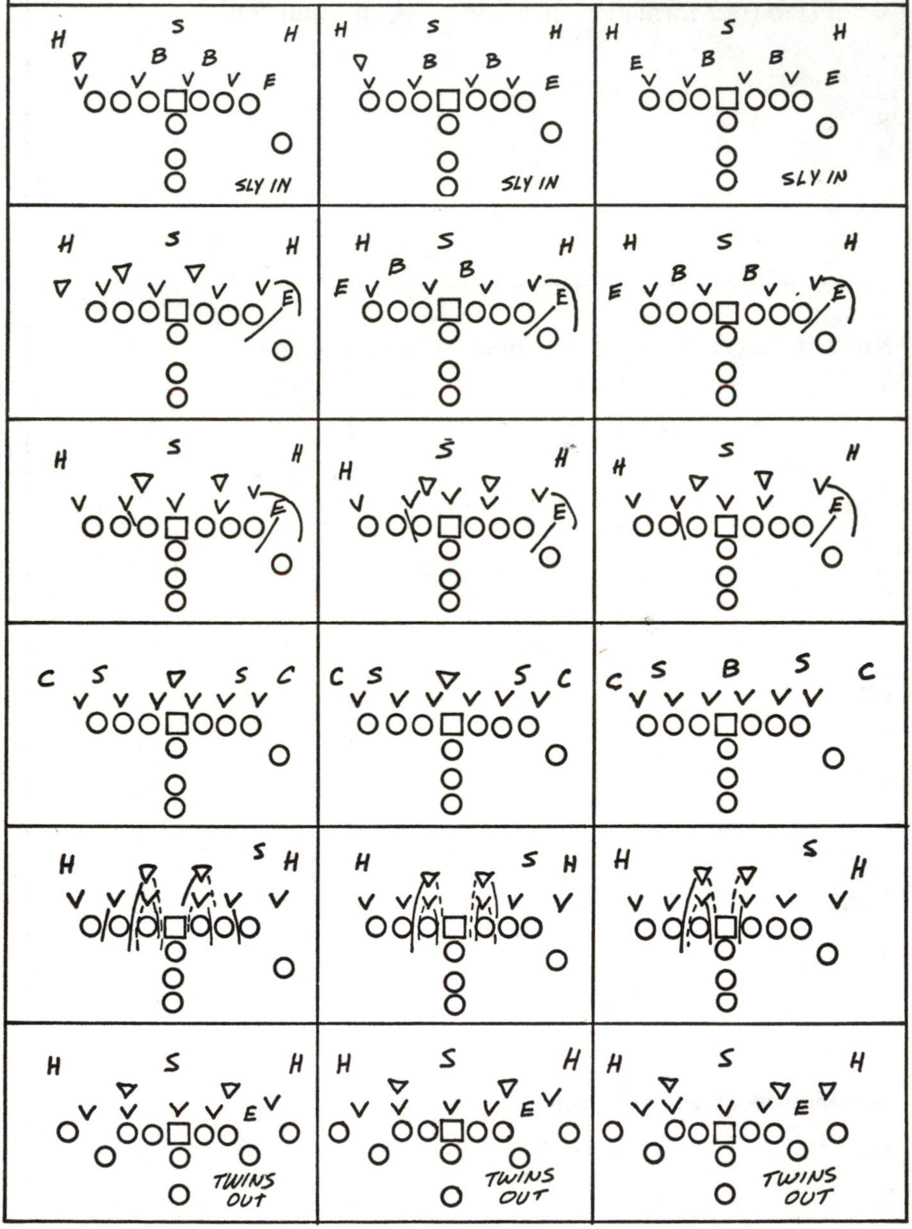

SLY IN

SLY IN

SLY IN

TWINS OUT

TWINS OUT

TWINS OUT

Diagram 12-8

SCOUT REPORT TEST

(Fill out after viewing opponent's film, if available.)

NAME _____ DATE _____ OPPONENT _____

1. Describe their kickoff (or kickoff return).

2. Detail their punt return (or punt).

3. Give any notes on their PAT/FG (or PAT/FG defense).

4. Give number and position of key offensive players (or defensive player).

5. Give the important offensive notes (or defensive).

6. Give their major offensive sets (or defensive).

7. Give their plays we must stop (or defensive adjustments we must beat).

8. Give your personal observations about your specific opponent.

Diagram 12-9

GAME REMINDERS' TEST

NAME ——————DATE ————— OPPONENT ——————

1. List units (Depth Chart) you are on (and first or substitute).

2. List important position (O and D) reminders for you personally.

3. List important kicking reminders (O and D) for you personally.

Diagram 12-10

13

How You Can Become an Organized Tactician

THERE IS NOTHING more distressing to a coach than watching a great offense or great talent flounder when it is obvious it should be rolling to victory. You may ask yourself how this can happen to a group that has so much going for it. Usually it boils down to poor decisions in moments of crisis. When a split-second decision is required, the wrong one is made, and the day is lost. Every coach has to live with the sportswriter who has the liberty to go back to his or her office and ponder the decision that may have turned victory into defeat, or the Monday morning quarterback who three days later wants to know why you did (or didn't do) this or that. The critics will be there forever, but their chance to criticize your failures will be much less frequent if you don't have to make too many critical decisions on impulse.

Proper organization can save many a day that is waiting to go either way. You can no doubt name several teams or programs that win far more often than they seem capable of. What is the ingredient that creates victory when the players don't seem to have the ability? The victors are just *too well prepared* to be beaten. This comment is often made in reference to Don Shula's Miami Dolphins. Though their talent does not seem to match up all the time, they usually win the game they're not supposed to. In the media postmortems, their continued success is credited to Shula's organization and planning.

In an average football game there are nine or ten plays that will decide the outcome of the game, and you only have six time-outs. That means approximately four of those critical decisions must be made on the spur of the moment. If you make the wrong choice, there is no second chance. Therefore, the key to continued success lies in being prepared for any eventuality and being able to make all major decisions quickly, based on all the information available.

Many decisions can be made in the off-season, and some during game week at planning meetings. Other decisions, however, must be made during the heat of battle when the coach is under maximum stress.

If the game is going according to plan, the coach can rely on decisions made after days of statistical evaluation. But in tight ball games the element of surprise and the strange bounce of the ball must be built into the plan. Total organization that catalogs everything and has it at your fingertips will make the difference between mediocrity and constant success. This requires an intelligence gathering system that can plot the flow of the game and provide the coach with all the information necessary to make his decisions from analysis instead of passion.

An important key in eliminating tactical errors is in proper staff utilization. Each coach on the staff must be able to disect some phase of the game as it unfolds and use necessary adjustments quickly so the flow of each attack is not interrupted. Following is a plan that may help eliminate some of the tactical errors that stop the best of teams.

PRESS-BOX ORGANIZATION

A minimum of two coaches is needed to handle the offensive strategy in the press box; both coaches will develop charts as the game unfolds. Most of the charts have been prepared prior to the start of the game. The opponent's tendencies and defensive sequences have been broken down and listed on the proper charts.

The first chart needed is the opponent's personnel chart (see Chart 13-1). This chart will be drawn up from the scouting report. When the defense lines up for the first play, each number must be checked to see if it corresponds with the scouting report; if any numbers are different, the change is noted immediately. This will save time following substitutes coming and going from the field of play.

The second chart is the Play-Call Chart (see Diagram 13-2). It, too, is developed from the scouting report. In the scouting report you will chart all the opponent's defenses by down, distance, hash-mark, field position, and game situation. After analyzing their tendencies, the coaching staff will select the best play to attack the anticipated defense in every down and distance situation. Enter the game with only one choice when the game is even and one choice when you are behind and time is becoming a factor. If the scouting report shows the opponent has a tendency to use several defenses and you are not sure which one you will see, prepare a chart for each defense. Each square of the chart will list the best information, the blocking scheme or motion (if needed), and the play.

In the preparation of this chart, you will rely heavily on your opponent's past reactions to you. That is why you must keep thorough records

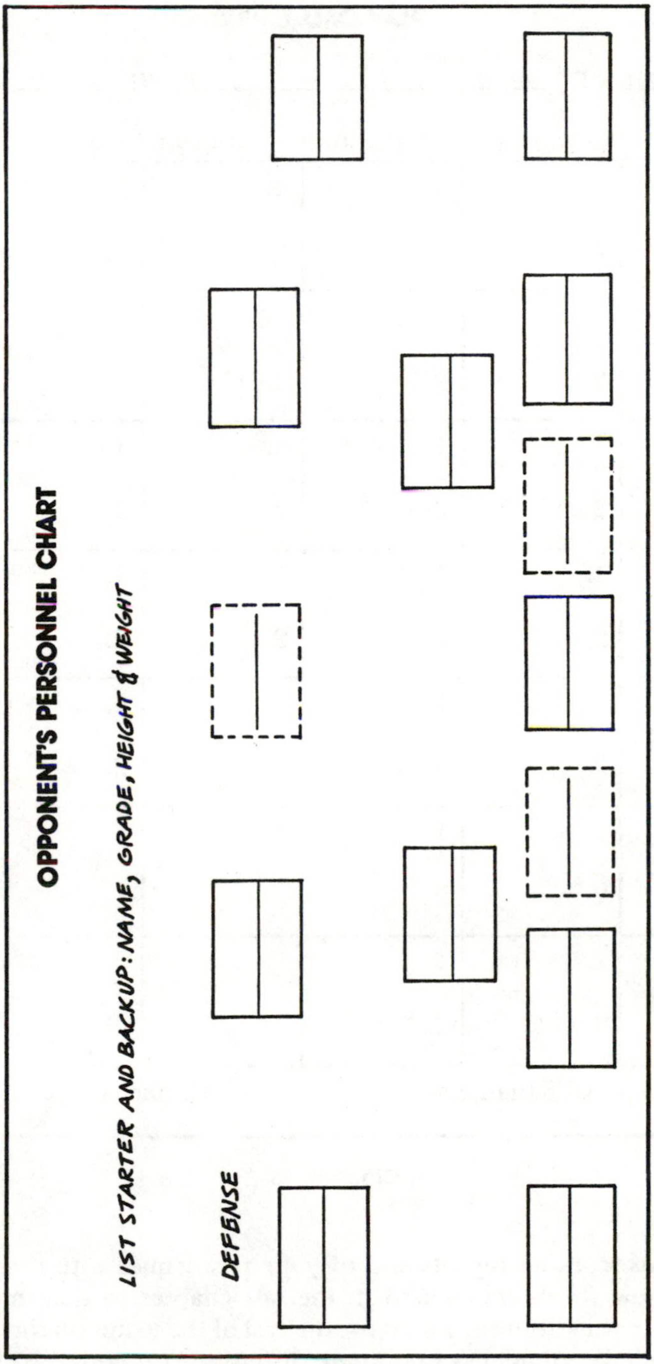

OPPONENT'S PERSONNEL CHART

LIST STARTER AND BACKUP: NAME, GRADE, HEIGHT & WEIGHT

DEFENSE

Diagram 13-1

PLAY-CALL CHART

OPPONENT ————————————————————— YEAR —————————

	(G+9)	10–39)	(−40–20)	(−20–G)	
1/10	1. 2.	1. 2.	1. 2.	1. 2.	1/10
2/Long	1. 2.	1. 2.	1. 2.	1. 2.	2/L
2/Short	1. 2.	1. 2.	1. 2.	1. 2.	2/S
3/Long 3/L	1. 2.	1. 2.	1. 2.	1. 2.	3/L
3/Short	1. 2.	1. 2.	1. 2.	1. 2.	3/S
4/Long	1. 2.	1. 2.	1.		4/L
4/Short	1. 2.	1. 2.	1.		4/S

Special Situations   Two-Minute Attack

Diagram 13–2

of previous scouting reports and of your past games with them. Use the game review sheets mentioned in the last chapter to determine if they prepare for you differently than for the rest of the teams on their schedule. If they do have a tendency to prepare differently for you, this chart will be developed more from your previous experience with this opponent than from their tendencies against teams played in the few weeks prior to your

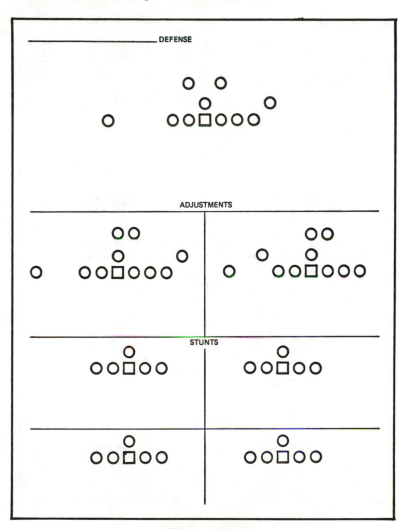

Diagram 13-3a

game. This chart will also list special-situation plays. You may also list a series of choices for waste-down plays (second and one, etc.).

The master scouting book is always taken to the press box, permitting you to have everything they have ever shown handy in the event of an unusual situation. Especially important are the master defensive pages (see Diagrams 13-3a and 13-3b). These forms will give you a quick breakdown on every defense the opponent has ever shown, with all the stunts and adjustments. But on game day the most important part of this form is the backside. Here you list the plays that have proven most successful against that opponent when they were using that defense. Also keep an abbreviated booklet on how to attack every defense (a synopsis of each chapter in this book) in the press box.

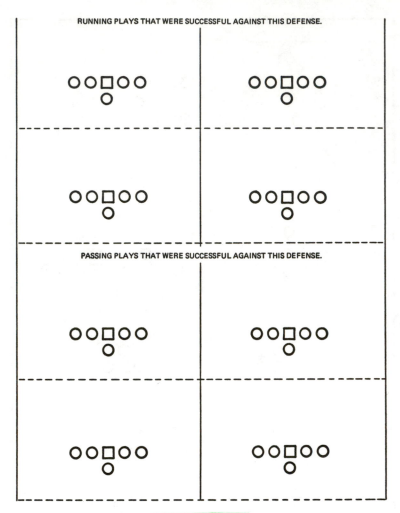

RUNNING PLAYS THAT WERE SUCCESSFUL AGAINST THIS DEFENSE.

PASSING PLAYS THAT WERE SUCCESSFUL AGAINST THIS DEFENSE.

Diagram 13-3b

The other charts must be developed as the game progresses. The coach who is most concerned with play selection will keep a Play Selection Chart (see Diagram 13-4). Each time a play is called, this coach will list the formation used, the direction ran, and the result. To the right of each choice he will note the defender that made first contact with the ballcarrier. By referring to the personnel chart he can quickly determine the original position of the tackler. With his knowledge of your blocking scheme he can immediately determine if the defense outsmarted your blocking scheme or if the tackler defeated your blocker. By charting in this manner, trends will appear as the game progresses. If the same player makes the tackle each time you run a specific play, you must either change the blocking scheme or

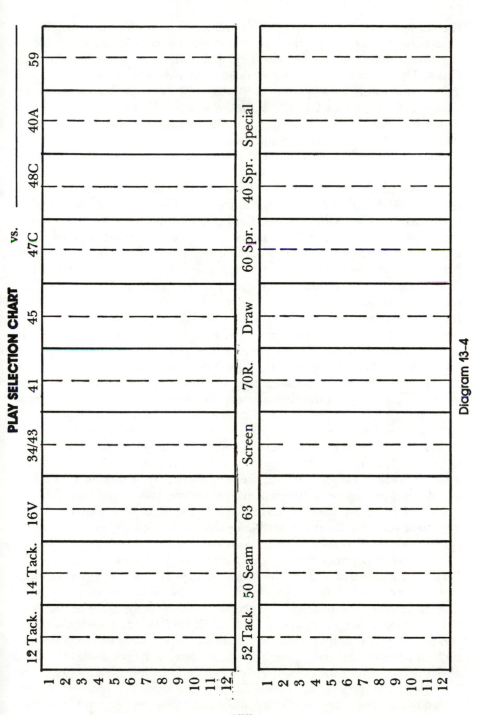

PLAY SELECTION CHART

vs.

12 Tack. 14 Tack. 16V 34/43 41 45 47C 48C 40A 59

1
2
3
4
5
6
7
8
9
10
11
12

52 Tack. 50 Seam 63 Screen 70R. Draw 60 Spr. 40 Spr. Special

1
2
3
4
5
6
7
8
9
10
11
12

Diagram 13-4

155

the blocker assigned that player. It will be this coach's responsibility to determine the necessary adjustment. If there is to be a formation or blocking adjustment, each coach will then make the change on his Play Call Chart. The coach will constantly evaluate your play selections for consistent gainers and losers. If a play is not averaging 4 yards per carry, the coach should go to your Play Call Chart, note the places that call is scheduled to be used in the future, and suggest a replacement play. He can also readily note those plays that are having success and place more of those high-consistency plays in more frequently used spots during late stages of the game.

The other coach in the press box fills in a chart of the defense's plays by Down and Distance (see Diagram 13-5). You will note this chart is further divided by hash-mark and field position; specifically it is divided by four-down zones or three-down zones. If you had any additional defensive breakdown, there would be too many categories to notice any trends. In preparation of the game plan, the offensive Play Call Chart is developed from a similar chart gleened from the scouting report tendencies. So when the game starts, the first thing you need to know is whether they are following the pattern established in the scouting report or a newly developed special pattern for your game. If they are following a new pattern, what has caused them to alter their philosophy? Are they defending by down and distance, horizontal field position, or formation?

If you are the coach developing this chart, you must make a major decision by the end of the first quarter. Have they changed their defense from the scouting report? If it is the same, you should continue with your game plan as designed, making only the changes that the other spotter sees necessary for the continued development of your game plan. But if the defense is different from the one you anticipated, immediate adjustments must be made. As already noted, these changes may be a pattern of stunts you did not anticipate, a different pass coverage, special personnel alterations that may affect your attacking strategy, or new people that you may want to attack. The latter two problems should still be handled by the other spotter, but the former should be your concern.

A bad experience caused the authors of this book to institute the Personnel Placement Chart. We faced an opponent a few years ago that had one very good defensive halfback, while the other one was very poor. The game plan called for us to concentrate our passing game at the weak defender and avoid the good one. At the half-time meeting, we found these two people had switched sides. This explains why we had just experienced such an unsuccessful half. Thus you should have your personnel classified after the first play of the game to protect yourself from such a foolish error.

If your opponent has a favorite stunting situation, have a play designed to beat the anticipated stunt and write it into your script. If the chart shows they have abandoned that stunt or are using it in another situation, shift your play call to complement their change.

DEFENSE BY DOWN AND DISTANCE

Opponent _____   Year _____

1 AND 10

Left	Middle	Right
Def. Stun. Res.	Def. Stun. Res.	Def. Stun. Res.

2 AND SHORT

Left	Middle	Right
Def. Stun. Res.	Def. Stun. Res.	Def. Stun. Res.

3 AND SHORT

Left	Middle	Right
Def. Stun. Res.	Def. Stun. Res.	Def. Stun. Res.

2 AND LONG

Left	Middle	Right
Def. Stun. Res.	Def. Stun. Res.	Def. Stun. Res.

3 AND LONG

Left	Middle	Right
Def. Stun. Res.	Def. Stun. Res.	Def. Stun. Res.

4th

Left	Middle	Right
Def. Stun. Res.	Def. Stun. Res.	Def. Stun. Res.

3 down zone 4 down zone 3 down zone 4 down zone 3 down zone 4 down zone

4 down zone 3 down zone 4 down zone 3 down zone 4 down zone 3 down zone

T T T T T T

Diagram 13–5

The most significant contribution you can make is to determine whether they have entered the game with a totally new defensive strategy. If this is the case, refer immediately to the master scouting book to find out if they have shown this defense before. Usually the defense that is used to surprise you is something they have played in the past. Turn to the backside of that form to check the plays you have seen work against that look. Where changes are needed, work quickly on your Play Call Chart, placing the revisions in the appropriate blocks; specifically, note what passes should be changed and what is the best blocking scheme and formation for the option, or the best blocking scheme for the inside plays. If this page does not give enough information, then revert to your booklet on each defense, which is a synopsis of everything listed in this book.

SIDELINE ORGANIZATION

On the sideline the team statistician will keep a running account of the game on a Game Sequence Chart (see Diagram 13–6). This chart will show in an instant why the offensive drives are unsuccessful. Too often you may get so engrossed in a game that you lose perspective of why you are getting bogged down. You start to make drastic changes in the game plan when the circumstances don't suggest a change in strategy. It may be penalties, fumbles, or interceptions that keep the offense from scoring. This may require changing personnel rather than changing the offense.

After the game is over, this chart will be used more than any other. It is needed for the film review as well as for a complete understanding of the flow of the game. This will be important in developing your long-range philosophy.

The coach on the sideline who calls the plays should be in constant phone contact with the spotter keeping the play selection chart. If the selection about to be sent in has been showing poor results, the coach with this chart will see it immediately and should recommend an alternate choice. He should also be ready to offer an alternate formation or blocking method if the opponent has been beating the current scheme.

At the end of each offensive series, the coach will meet with the offensive unit when they come off the field. There should be assigned seats on the bench for this group to eliminate confusion in finding one another on the crowded sideline. Paint the offensive and defensive bench different colors to make the meeting place easier to locate. The first thing to be discussed is the defensive alignment. Together with the spotters, the bench coach reviews the defense with the players to verify that the players and coaches are seeing the same thing. Then they review the stunts that transpired during the series by referring to the specific play when the stunt occurred.

Next you want the players to assess the strengths and weaknesses of the people playing opposite them. Ask them to tell you where they think they can run most effectively. It is human nature for a player not to admit defeat, so you seldom want to ask the players where they cannot run. But the players will tell you which is the best side to run a particular play. This is an advantage of flip-flopping the line. Each lineman samples the defensive strength on either side and is able to give you an educated opinion on the direction each play should be run.

Once these matters are settled, ask the players how they want to block each hole and review with them the suggestions of the coaches in the press box.

When you have settled the group problems, the spotters will talk with individual players that are responsible for your blocking breakdowns. The coach upstairs should be able to offer specific technique revisions that will improve the blocker's success ratio.

At the end of the series, the quarterback should meet with the coach calling the plays. The coach and quarterback should share reactions on what happened on the field to insure that both are on the same wave length. When the coaches in the box are free, they should talk to the quarterback. He needs to know if they defend the option differently from what was practiced. If so, he needs to know what the new reads are. The coaches also review with him the pass coverage and where to expect pressure when he sets up to throw.

The coaches will consult with the players following each series. The team gets a very positive additional benefit from this. After his evaluation of the situation on the field is solicited, each player begins to assume the role of a coach in his own area. And when the players feel they are contributing to the game plan, their desire to succeed becomes greater because a loss will reflect on their decisions as well as on the coaches'. The attitude that the players and coaches are "all in this together" creates a family atmosphere that will carry you through those tense periods.

HALF-TIME

Proper use of the fifteen minutes at half-time can spell the difference between victory and defeat. When your staff reaches the locker room, you should all have a solid understanding of the opponent's defensive game plan and be prepared to make the necessary adjustments to thwart that plan. You must organize and simplify this information so the meeting with the squad will quickly clarify your offensive intentions and solidify every player's understanding of your objectives for the final half.

While the players are refreshing themselves, the coaches meet to review the first-half statistics on the Sequence, Down and Distance, and Play Selection Charts. Each coach should have reached some positive or negative conclusion on the various phases of your plan; this may require some alteration in the original game plan. The charts will show these trends and

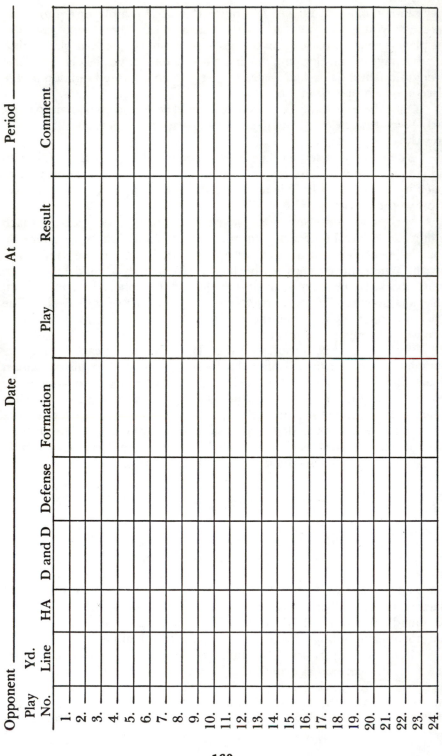

GAME SEQUENCE CHART

Opponent _____ Date _____ At _____ Period _____

Play No.	Yd. Line	HA	D and D	Defense	Formation	Play	Result	Comment
1.								
2.								
3.								
4.								
5.								
6.								
7.								
8.								
9.								
10.								
11.								
12.								
13.								
14.								
15.								
16.								
17.								
18.								
19.								
20.								
21.								
22.								
23.								
24.								

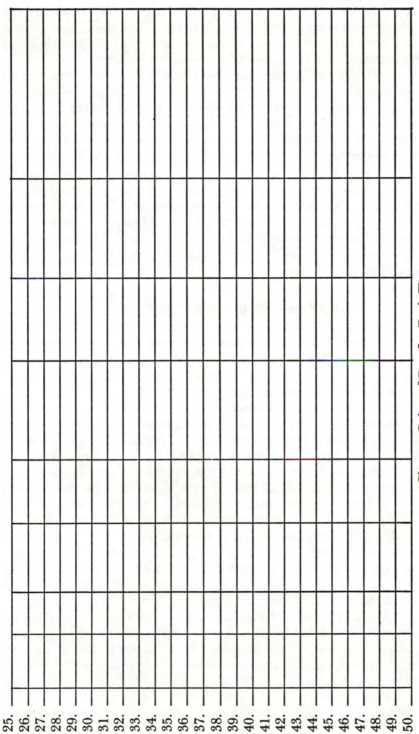

Change Color of Pen for Each Team

Diagram 13–6 (cont'd)

they should be discussed at this time. Eliminate from the second half the game plan blocking schemes or plays that are not working, and replace them with plays that have proven successful in the first half, provided they will be consistent with the opponent's defensive tendencies.

Next, after reviewing the opponent's tackle chart, make decisions on your players. Should you make personnel changes, blocking adjustments, or technique changes to neutralize the defenders giving you the most trouble? Once these decisions have been made, it is time to meet with the squad.

The spotter in charge of charting the enemy's defense will have prepared a transparency for use on the overhead projector showing their alignment by jersey number. This will save several minutes of argument on the location of the defenders. In fact, if there are inaccuracies, all eleven offensive players will start shouting simultaneously. This allows you to quickly get on with the more important matters. Explain to the squad all the changes that will be needed to keep the offense on the move. Then open the meeting to the players for individual questions and suggestions on your proposed strategy.

PLAY CALLING IN THE BELLY OPTION

There is no set guide to play calling because of the many variables that affect each decision. You must prepare your own guide to play calling after evaluating the possibilities. But there are some basic points to consider each time you organize your play-calling strategy. Below are all the factors you must weigh prior to making those choices.

When classifying offensive plays, divide them into two general categories. One category is the high-consistency gainers and the other is the low-consistency plays. The mark of consistency is determined by the amount of time a particular play gains 4 yards or better. If a play averages better than 4 yards per carry at least 55 percent of the time, classify it as a high-consistency play. Every play mentioned in this book has an overall average of 4 yards per carry. If you find a play averaging less than that over a reasonable period of time, drop it from the offense.

Let's take a few moments to clarify just what it means to average 4 yards per carry. The belly-arc pass to the slotback is completed about 65 percent of the time for an average gain of 16 yards per completion. This means that the play is a high-consistency gainer with an average per attempt of close to 12 yards. Meanwhile, the wingback-scissors play has an overall average of 6.8 yards per attempt, but its consistency rate is only about 44 percent. This means the play will be stopped for little gain 56 percent of the time, but the other times it is run the yardage is tremendous, thus balancing the statistics. This is not a play you want to run on third and two but a worthwhile selection on third and twelve.

Each play can also vary in its consistency rating from defense to defense. The arc pass is almost unstoppable against a gap-eight defense, while it becomes a very poor risk against a five-under-zone pass defense. When reviewing the earlier chapters you should note the times a play is classified a low-consistency or high-consistency choice. The coach should prepare a chart before starting any play-calling strategy. In one column, list all the high-consistency gainer plays (plays that are steady gainers and offer little chance of losing yardage), and in another column the plays that may lose 5 yards one time but break the game wide open the next.

Vertical Field Zones

Own Goal to Own 20 Yard Line:

1. Run high-consistency plays, especially traps.
2. Throw only high-consistency passes and only when the defense dictates pass.

Own 20 to Opponent's 40 Yard Line:

1. Run every play that goes against a particular defense.
2. Feature short passes that permit ball control.
3. Use low-consistency plays as situations dictate.
4. Use big plays and trick plays after you cross the 35 yard line. First down is a good time.

Opponent's 40 to Opponent's 10 Yard Line:

1. Use passes and counters on waste downs (2nd and 1, etc.) and on first down.
2. On all other downs run high-consistency plays to get another first down.

Goal Line:

1. Show a new formation; make the defense concentrate on adjustments.
2. Stress man-blocking schemes.
3. Stress plays that require the minimum amount of ball handling.

Run-or-Pass Decisions

Whether you run or pass should be a secondary choice. Whether you should use a high-consistency or low-consistency play is more important. Generally, passes fall into the low-consistency category, along with the counters and game specials (see Chapter 11). The option and fullback dives are usually high-consistency plays. So, in preparing a game plan you should not be thinking run or pass as much as you should be thinking rate of consistency.

Motivating the Offense

THE BEST MOTIVATOR of any offense should be the success of the offense itself. An offense such as the belly option that scores frequently will provide much of the inspiration to the offensive personnel, who will be anxious to keep it rolling. This pride in programs developed through success is an invaluable side effect.

Coaches with programs that are proven winners over a long period of time have usually developed successful motivational approaches which have kept them on the winning track. The motivation techniques used should be well thought out, planned, practiced, and believed by the coaches. There is nothing more transparent than a fake motivational technique.

INDIVIDUAL MOTIVATION

Certainly the most desired motivation is self-motivation. When an individual is driven from within, he will provide himself with the needed stimulus to keep striving for the goal. Unfortunately, most players are not self-motivated; the coach should be on the lookout for those young men on his squad who are, as these players are the real winners. They should not be taken for granted, but be continually fueled with thoughts that will keep them inspired. Place constant emphasis on the importance of your athletes to keep self-motivated.

In working toward this objective, each player should be encouraged to set individual goals. This goal setting can take place at a formal meeting between you and your players. Prior to the meeting, the coaching staff will evaluate each player using the form shown in Diagram 14–1. Each coach will fill out an evaluation chart on every player. The totals are averaged out and the player is shown his average rating in each category. These evaluations are done three times a year and kept in each player's file.

When you and your player sit down to discuss his personal goals, the evaluation chart serves as a good starting point. Point out his various strengths and weaknesses, using them to motivate the athlete toward his personal goals. After his goals are formulated, he should be encouraged to develop a plan of attack for reaching each goal. Naturally, this plan should

PLAYER EVALUATION FORM

Name _____ Grade _____

Circle the score you feel most fits the player in each of the following subject areas.

	Grade	7	8	9	10	11
1. Experience in playing school football		½	½	1	regular 2	2
					substitute 1	1

		Poor	Fair	Average	Good	Excellent
2. Size and Speed (in track equipment)						
Excellent 10.5 or less	Under 150		0	1	2	3
Good—10.6 to 11.2	150–175		1	2	3	4
Average—11.3 to 11.8	175–200		1	3	4	5
Fair—11.9 and up	200–up		1	3	5	6
3. Knowledge of position		0	1	1	2	3
4. Agility to tumble and react		0	1	1	2	5
5. Desire to play		0	1	2	4	5
6. Ability to learn (football)		0	1	1	2	3
7. Attitude toward coaches and players		0	0	1	2	3
8. Leadership qualities		0	0	1	2	3
9. Guts		0	0	1	2	3

TOTAL POINTS _____

	Seniors	Juniors	Sophomores	Freshmen
1. Excellent	25 & up	23 & up	22 & up	21 & up
2. Good	20 to 24	18 to 22	17 to 21	16 to 20
3. Average	16 to 19	14 to 17	13 to 16	12 to 15
4. Fair	14 to 15	12 to 13	11 to 12	10 to 11
5. Poor	0 to 13	0 to 11	0 to 10	0 to 9

Diagram 14-1

have time constraints and you can be helpful in establishing the proper course of action. Goals are not usually attained overnight, and you can assist your player in not only determining the time frame for reaching his goal, but also in the steps necessary for obtaining it. Use the step ladder method in setting long-term goals. For example, a freshman player may desire to become an "all-conference" performer. But you know this player is at least three years away from the objective. Rather than being totally negative and saying "no way," you should take the positive approach and tell him how his goal is possible by his junior year, then outline for him the steps (ladder) necessary to reach this goal. At this point in the interview, suggestions should be solicited from the player with guidance from you on how to reach a goal. These might include the following: practice hard every day; learn all I can about my job; make great strides in off-season programs; be a starter as a sophomore; be a good leader; and be a standout performer as a junior. This sample list of steps, when climbed one at a time, will enable the individual to reach his "all-conference" goal.

It is imperative to stress team goals when working with individual goals. After all, every coach knows "team" comes before "individual," but to the individual, it will often be "me first." Favor the approach that helps the individual realize that his personal goals can be obtained through the team. For example, the player desiring to become "all-conference" has a much better chance of reaching that goal if his team is the conference champion. Hence, team goals of conference champions can become very important to this individual. When he understands this "individual goals through team goals" approach, he will be more receptive to team goals.

Self-motivation will flourish best in an atmosphere in which each person believes he is good and is getting better all the time. When a squad believes it is a winner, both collectively and individually, it is amazing how much it can accomplish. It becomes extremely confident and develops an almost cocky air. This latter trait can be toned down by the mentor as needed. Each coach on your staff should foster the idea "we are good" and should avoid negatism in all coaching. Even if a player needs chewing out, do it in a positive manner that does not discourage him, but instead pressures him to improve. You will be amazed by the positive results obtained through this approach.

This approach of visualism or positive self-image should be stressed regularly and each phase of this approach should be planned before it is presented to the players. In the end, you want your players to view themselves as successful. The enthusiasm of the coaching staff is vital in fostering all aspects of motivation.

TEAM MOTIVATION

To keep the offense operating at peak efficiency, always look for new methods that will produce the needed inspiration. These methods are always subject to change if they don't work or if you find something that sparks your squad more. An awards system could be a must for you. Use the following methods to motivate your offense with great success.

Select the Players of the Week based on film grade and performance factors as judged by the position coaches. Each player selected has his name and photograph placed on the chart in the locker room on Tuesday (Diagram 14–2), his picture placed on the award bulletin board near the student cafeteria on Wednesday, and receives a certificate designating his

---

FOOTBALL STANDOUTS

DELAWARE VALLEY

JUNIATA

JOHNS HOPKINS

(List All Names Selected)

Diagram 14–2

accomplishments on Friday (Diagram 14–3). His accomplishments are published in the weekly awards release on Thursday and his accomplishments and picture are placed in the next home game program. In addition, one of the area players of the week is selected the Team Player of the Week by a vote of the coaching staff (Diagram 14–4).

Also, have a Winners Chart for all players grading 80 percent or more (see Diagram 14–5). This chart shows the consistent performers who are so vital to the offensive success. The chart is derived by grading every offensive player's performance, play-by-play, during past game film review. Use a plus-minus system. A plus is awarded when the player successfully carries out his assignment and a minus if he fails. The end result of this task is the Offensive Grade Report (Diagram 14–6) which is the basis for the Winner's Chart. These awards are great for public relations and players love them, especially when they are doing well.

The Offensive Goals Chart (Diagram 14–7) gives everyone an opportunity to see the offensive musts accomplished during the game in question. It also gives an indication of the offensive success of each game.

The list of goals is decided upon before the start of each season. If you accomplish all of the goals, you will win. In fact, if you succeed in reaching most of the goals you should win. Try to make the attainment of these goals important to your team. For achieving five of the 12 goals, award all regular members (20 players or more) of the offensive squad a star. Five checks earned is the minimum aim. If ten goals are attained, then two stars are presented. This usually results in a win, as already mentioned. A three-star award is given if all 12 goals are reached. This emphasis on team achievements is in keeping with your team-before-self theory. Winning is your goal and is required for any award to be presented. Always emphasize team consistency, since consistency leads to success. This approach certainly gives winning top priority.

In addition to the Team Offensive Stars system, have an individual Offensive Goals (star) Program (Diagram 14–8) for every player participating in 20 or more plays. This enables you to emphasize both the achievements of the individual and the team as well. Remember, no awards are made unless you win. This again keeps the emphasis of the awards system on team success. These awards are given out on game day during the pre-game team meeting.

Outstanding Achievement

Widener University

Football Citation

Presented to _____

For _____

Football Recognition

FOOTBALL PLAYER OF THE WEEK

DELAWARE VALLEY _____

JUNIATA _____

JOHNS HOPKINS _____

(List the Selected Player)

Diagram 14–4

OFFENSIVE "WINNERS"

Grade 80% or More

	LT	LG	C	RG	RT	TE	SB	SE	RB	RB	QB

DELAWARE VALLEY _____

JUNIATA _____

JOHNS HOPKINS _____

(List All Players Who Attain Goal)

Diagram 14–5

You will note from the chart that there are four goals for the individual to attain. Two are film grade percentages and the latter two are for superior effort as determined by the offensive coaching staff.

Here, individual consistency is stressed; in addition, place emphasis on individuals rising above the expected performance and making the big play. The individual is awarded a star if he receives a mark in any two individual categories; three marks result in two stars, and if all four marks are received, he is awarded three stars.

In conclusion, this approach is recognition via winning, with consideration for team performance, individual consistency, and individual excellence. All three of these areas are to be stressed in an offensive-awards system.

FILM GRADE REPORT FORMS

Player	Plays	Plays Graded	Grade	Comments

Overall Area Comments:

_____

_____

Diagram 14–6

OFFENSIVE GOALS' CHART

(Check Each Goal Attained;

opponents' names to head columns.)

TEAM OFFENSIVE GOALS	Team Offensive Stars		
5 offensive touchdowns			
no sacks (at least 8 or more attempts)			
Score 100% inside opposing 10 yard line			
Only forced to punt 4 times or less			
10 play drive or more (and score or good field position) (2 times)			
2 or less turnovers and none in our territory			
200 yards or more rushing			
100 yards or more passing			
300 yards or more total offense			
40% pass completion average			
Defense receives good field position (inside their 35–4 times or more)			
50% success on all 3rd down situations			
TOTAL			

Must win game for awards

Must play 20 or more plays (Coaches' discretion)

5 checks = 1 star; 10 = 2; 12 = 3

Diagram 14-7

INDIVIDUAL OFFENSIVE STARS
AND
INDIVIDUAL OFFENSIVE GOALS

NAME	80%	90%	BIG PLAY 1	BIG PLAY 2	SUB-TOTAL	TEAM STARS

List players' names and check each goal attained.

Diagram 14-8

RECORD KEEPING FOR MOTIVATION

Keep the usual offensive statistics, both team and individual, and emphasize those stats that will motivate the offensive players and unit. You want to recognize team and individual leaders in the Conference, and if applicable, in national categories. The value of these stats is further enhanced during recruiting. Student athlete recruiters have told us our starter's recognition has been a factor in their interest in our program. One running back, in particular, indicated his desire to play in our program because the running back always had high yardage per carry stats.

Also keep stats to help motivate the coaching staff. These stats (Diagrams 14-9, 14-10, and 14-11) are invaluable to planning your attack. The offensive staff is usually able to recognize just where you stand in terms of the offense's progress.

The Game Sequence and Play Call Charts (see Chapter 13) present you with a self-scouting look at your play calling. You can check all calls in particular situations plus each play's success factor. The Game Sequence Chart shows the results of each offensive possession and the staff receives a visual, statistical picture of the total offensive results for the game. Also, the Possession and Turnover Chart is an invaluable tool that further expands the Game Sequence Chart, while emphasizing the turnover problem. These charts allow the staff a look at the items imperative to your offensive success. These stats give you the impetus to strive to keep your offense in high gear.

DOWN AND DISTANCE CHART

D and D	Y.L.	PLAY	RES	E/I	NO	D and D	Y.L.	PLAY	RES	E/I	NO	D and D	Y.L.	PLAY	RES E/I

Diagram 14–9

DRIVE CHART

NUMBER	START	PLAYS	FINISH	FIRSTS	LENGTH	RESULT	NET	COMMENTS

Diagram 14-10

POSSESSIONS AND TURNOVERS

Offense

	Field Zone Area					
	Our Goal line to −35		−35 to +35		+35 to Opp.'s Goal line	
	Game	Season	Game	Season	Game	Season
Fumbles Lost						
Passes Intercepted						
Stopped on Downs						
Forced to Punt						
Missed Field Goal						
TOTALS						

	Game	Season
Time Ran Out		
Scored		
Total Possessions		
Scoring Percentage		

	Game	Season
Total Fumbles Lost & Passes Intercepted		
Number that led to Opponent's Scores		

Diagram 14–11

The Total Efficiency Chart (Diagram 14–12), the Efficiency Chart (Diagram 14–13), and the Visual Play Chart (Diagram 14–14) play an important role in your play-calling selection and are invaluable tools in structuring the offense. The Total Efficiency Chart presents a synopsis of your efficiency, game by game and area by area; the Efficiency Chart gives a look at the results of each individual running and passing play; and the Visual Play Chart further shows each play run during the game. These also help in designing your offensive plans each year as well as in formulating the weekly game plan.

TOTAL EFFICIENCY CHART

Totals

PLAYS	EFF	I	BIG	BAD	%	PLAYS	EFF	I	BIG	BAD	%
R U N											
P A S S											
S P E C I A L S											
T O T A L											

Diagram 14–12

EFFICIENCY CHART

G	ATT	NET	EFF	G	ATT	NET	EFF	G	ATT	NET	EFF
		TOTAL				TOTAL				TOTAL	
	ATT	NET	EFF		ATT	NET	EFF		ATT	NET	EFF

Diagram 14–13

VISUAL PLAY CHART

Team ——————————— Date ———————————

L = Left
R = Right

Run Game

Speed		Dream		Option		Scissors		Counter Speed		Counter option		Sneak	
L	R	L	R	L	R	L	R	L	R	L	R	L	R

Pass Game

Speed		Dream		Counter						Roll	
L	R	L	R	L	R					L	R

Diagram 14–14

178

15

How to Teach
Belly Option Offense

LIKE ANY OFFENSE, the belly teams use standard teaching drills, but there are some drills that are more specifically designed to facilitate the teaching of this style of attack. Listed in this chapter are the drills that are most important to the development of this offense. The proper teaching method, the equipment needed, and the time necessary to properly develop the individual skills are explained with each drill.

The value of practice sessions in the offense should be emphasized here. As a coach, you must understand your vital role as a teacher in the offense if the total offense is to succeed.

LINE SKILLS

The blocking drills have been organized to keep in tune with your blocking philosophy. Do not attempt to move your opponent, but to gain and maintain leverage for as long as possible.

Stance Drill

Equipment: Chalk Line.

Procedure: All your linemen are to stand with their feet shoulder-width apart on the chalk line. Each player is to place the heel of the forward foot on the line. Next, he is to place the toe of his back foot on the back edge of the line. If the toes are pointed straight ahead, each lineman should have proper foot alignment. Then from an elbows-on-knees position, each player is to rock forward until the weight is on the balls of the feet and complete the stance by letting both hands drop naturally until the fingertips touch the ground. The drill is concluded by having the players fire out 5 yards on command.

Techniques: The hands should be placed slightly in front and to the inside of the corresponding shoulder. The back should be parallel to the ground and the knees pointed straight ahead, not in. The heels should just clear the ground. The eyes are focused on the ground approximately three feet to the front, which will require the neck to be firm but not strained.

Coaching Points: Emphasize proper weight distribution. The weight should be equally distributed to all four points, except when fire blocking, which will require more weight placed on the hands. The coach should start at one end of the line and work his way down the line, correcting each stance as he goes. When each player has an acceptable stance, all of the players can be checked quickly by looking down the line, much as a drill sergeant would do when inspecting a column of troops.

Time: Fifteen minutes the first day. Five minutes the second day; then include with the Line Starts Drill.

Some coaches may question the necessity of such a formalized drill to teach the stance. But two points are of major consideration here. First is the time factor. You cannot have a confused or unorganized method of teaching the stance as it will take too long. Second, this is the first drill your players do each year; this drill more than any other must be efficient and military-like so the players begin to get a mental picture of good discipline and organization.

Line Starts Drill

Equipment: Seven-man blocking sled.

Procedure: The line is to assume a stance at arms length from the sled. After the stances have been checked, the line drives the sled 5 yards on command. After 5 yards the whistle is blown and the line will spin left or right off the sled on a signal from the manager riding the sled. The spin out serves two purposes. It forces the blockers to keep their heads up and neck bulled while blocking, and it quickly clears the sled for the next group.

Coaching Points: The coach should check for a straight line. Each blocker must keep a straight back while driving the sled. He cannot be permitted to turn his back into the pad in an attempt to get more leverage. Stress must be put on timing. Getting off on the count is vital.

Time: Five minutes each day until the skills listed in both preceding drills can be executed flawlessly. After the first week this drill is included with the Formations Drill.

Formations Drill

Equipment: Seven-man sled.

Procedure: This drill is a progression of the Line Starts Drill. The line forms the preliminary pre-shift huddle alignment. The center initiates the drill by calling the huddle 5 yards behind the middle pad on the sled. As soon as the pre-shift huddle is formed, call the formation a mock play and break the huddle. The line is to turn out, form up, and advance to the sled.

At the line, count off the sled pads and get set. To assume the stance properly, each player places his hands even with the back edge of the ball, then adjusts his feet. As soon as the line is set, the coach gives the command to charge.

One ball is used in this drill. The center carries it into the huddle, then to the line of scrimmage. He snaps it to the center of the next group to block the sled. After the second center has taken the snap, he follows the sled as it is being driven by the first group. At the whistle he positions himself properly in front of the sled and calls the huddle for his group. This way there is no wasted motion and you can have each group complete the whole procedure from huddle to whistle in seconds.

Coaching Points: Stress is placed on proper position when the unit breaks from the huddle. The line should come to a complete stop 3 yards from the ball to find their count. After each man has counted, the line advances to the line of scrimmage. Watch the feet of the players as they get set. Often in their rush to get set they will not position their feet properly. Also, it is important that the group waiting to block form their huddle rapidly. A delay here causes the drill to drag out, thus limiting its value.

Time: Five minutes every day for three offensive lines; longer if more groups are participating. After the second week of practice this is a remedial drill.

Power Blocking Drill

Equipment: Weighted two-man sled.

Procedure: One blocker at a time will block the sled with his inside shoulder. Place a manager on the back end of the sled to make it immovable. On the starting command, the blocker is to drive the sled pad high in the air so that the whole front portion of the sled is off the ground. To do this, the blocker must use short chopping steps. Every player must power each pad twice before the drill is complete.

Coaching Points: By having the player drive the sled upward, he is required to use all the techniques needed to execute a proper block. His head must be up, his tail down, and his feet chopping in powerful steps. The coach must stress to the blocker the importance of driving his hips into the pad as he drives it upward.

Technique: A wide base is necessary for the blocker to control the sled. Each step is to be short; no single step should be longer than six inches. With each step, a gradual rise of the chest and shoulders is desired. The blocker must have his head up and eyes open looking at the treetops.

Time: It should take five minutes to have 15 blockers get the required number of reactions each day. As you get into the regular season, this drill becomes a warmup prepractice drill for every lineman.

Mule Team Drill

Equipment: Two-man blocking sled.

Procedure: Using the previously mentioned techniques, one or two players (as desired) are to drive an unweighted sled 10 yards. The blocker is to use short, chopping steps and drive the sled until the coach blows the whistle.

Coaching Points: If the sled swerves from side to side the blocker is not controlling it, due usually to a poor blocking base. If this is the case, stress must be placed on keeping a wide base. Later in the season, place two players 10 yards beyond the sled holding large lightweight dummies. On the whistle both blockers roll off the sled, then run to the dummies and throw a running downfield block, after which they become the dummy holders. This encourages your players to go for a second block after they have lost the first. See Diagram 15-1.

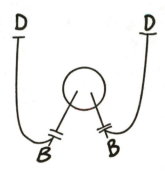

Diagram 15-1

Board Base Drill

Equipment: Three heavy stand-up dummies. Three 1 × 12 foot boards at least two inches thick. Blocking shute or high-jump standards and bar.

Procedure: Three blockers get set at the end of the board and on command fire down the board under the bar which is set in about four feet. Three players will hold large blocking dummies about half way down the board and offer some resistance to the blockers. The blockers must drive the bag to the other end of the board without stepping on it.

Coaching Points: If the coach will stand to the side of the three boards, he will be in good position to watch all three blockers at one time, provided that all three boards are lined up close together and parallel to one another. After the blocker can successfully drive the bag down the board, the board can be turned at various angles so the blocker can get the idea of angle-blocking. The dummy holder can be placed at varying distances down the board to simulate a lineman playing off the ball or a linebacker. As the blocker improves, the bag holder should offer more resistance until the blocker reaches a point where he is efficient enough to attack the defender without needing the bag. This is done about once a week on a competitive basis, with the blocker receiving a reward for not touching the board or being punished for stepping on it. After the third day, combine this drill with the Short Trap Drill.

Techniques: The blocker is to keep his head up, his tail down, and his eyes open. His back is to be arched and all his steps are to be no longer than six inches. Of course, the main point of the drill is to maintain a good blocking base, which should be pointed out to the blocker every time he steps on the board.

Time: Twenty blockers can accomplish the desired number of repetitions in about ten minutes if three players block at one time.

Commuter Drill

Equipment: None.

Procedure: This is a form-blocking drill designed to review all the various types of blocks each lineman has at his disposal. All the linemen are to be split into two parallel lines facing each other. A group of 20 is the most workable number.) One line is on offense and the other line serves as catcher; the coach is to position himself at the end of the blocking line. On command, the whole line will execute a specific block in the direction designated by the coach; then the other line follows suit by executing the same block.

Coaching Points: It is important that everyone move at top speed and that the defender catches only the blocker. Stress is placed on proper foot work and correct fundamentals. It is very easy for the coach to check all the players at once by watching from the end of the line. If one player moves incorrectly, he will stand out in the same way as a chorus line dancer who is out of time.

Technique: The footwork and proper blocking methods are described in Chapter 5. The blocks practiced in this drill are the Angle, Cutoff, On-Gap, Fire, Trap, Cup, Pick-off, and Linebacker.

Time: Spend five minutes every day of the season on this drill. Early in the season, when only a few of the blocks have been taught, have the players execute more repetitions of each block. But as the season progresses, review more blocks by doing less repetitions.

Explain to the players that this drill has considerable activity with many people moving, jostling, and bumping into one another, just as if they were on the commuter subway coming home from work. And like the daily commuter, about the only thing that will be hurt in this drill will be the catcher's feelings when someone bumps into him too hard.

A new block is added every day of practice until all eight blocks are in the blocker's repertoire. The block is always referred to by name and its component parts are reviewed daily.

This drill will be vital to your coaching system. You are not large enough to overpower most opponents, so you must attempt to beat them with technique. Place great stress upon knowing every block necessary to defeat the opponent. Each player must be able to transpose each segment of his particular rule into one of these eight blocks as soon as he locates the player he is to hit.

On-Gap Combat Drill

Equipment: Two long blocking boards and a banana pushback dummy for each group.

Procedure: Place two blocking boards in the shape of a "V" with the closed end about four feet apart. In the mouth of the "V" place a defender holding a banana pushback. The blocker is to assume a stance at the base of either board. On command, the blocker will attempt to on-gap block the defender in the "V." The blocker must step with his near foot and try to drive his head across the front of the defender in an attempt to stop the defender's penetration. As soon as contact is made, the blocker swings his hips around so he is facing upfield. By getting his hips around he will be able to create a stalemate. Since this is an aggressive block, the defender is to be driven upfield if possible.

The defender is to fight through the blocker's head with the dummy and is considered the winner if he is able to push the blocker outside the "V" shaped boundary. As the first blocker completes his action, the coach should turn to the other group who has gotten into position while the first player was blocking. After each player blocks he becomes the bag holder. By having two sets of boards there is no wasted motion and a good coach can accomplish up to ten reactions a minute.

Coaching Points: The defender is very important to the success of this drill. If he does not give maximum resistance, the on-gap blocker will not give his best effort and this difficult skill will never bear fruit in the game. The important part of the on-gap block is the swinging of the hips so the blocker is facing upfield. If this is not accomplished, the defender will easily fight through the head and be in immediate pursuit. The coach must also check the blocker's first step to be sure it is at least a foot long and aimed directly at the nose of the defender. Be sure the blocker uses his outside hand for leverage by grounding it as he blocks. Many players have a tendency to drop their heads when they cross the face of a defender. When the blocker's head goes down, so will the rest of his body, and he will never be able to drive the defender upfield. Finally, the coach is to constantly stress the importance of driving the far shoulder through the far knee of the defender.

Time: In early season a group of 12 players will spend 15 minutes a practice on the skill. Later in the year the time is cut to eight minutes and the number of reactions are cut in half.

Since this is the most difficult block in the offense, it must receive the most attention if it is to be used effectively.

Pass Block Drill

Equipment: Three tires.

Procedure: The offensive blocker sets up between the tires that represent the other linemen (see Diagram 15–2.) Three defensive players are placed across the line: one in the on-gap, one in the off-gap, and the third as a defensive end. The coach positions himself behind the offensive blocker at about a 4-yard depth, and he signals the defensive players he wishes to penetrate. On command, the designated defender attacks as the blocker must go through his pass-block maneuver to pick up the rusher. To make the drill competitive, time the pass blockers and reward the one that offers the coach the longest protection.

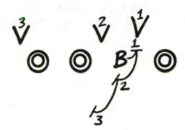

Diagram 15–2

Coaching Points: The coach must stress the importance of an aggressive on-gap step. It will enable the blocker to pick any hard charger in location number one. If this move is not aggressive, the attacker will bowl over the pass blocker. As the blocker completes the on-gap move, he will be in a crouched position, and it is important that he remain so throughout the rest of the pass-block procedure. If attacked on the cup technique, have the blocker use the hit-and-recoil maneuver. If neither number one nor number two attack, the blocker must shuffle into his own backfield and prepare to pick up any offside rusher. The pick-off is a screening maneuver unless the blocker is late in meeting the rusher. In this case you want the blocker to try and cut the defender down by diving in front of him.

Time: Your time requirements are the same for this drill as they were for the previous drill. In fact, you can run these two drills simultaneously by splitting your linemen into two equal groups.

Trap Step Drill

Equipment: Six 2-by-6-inch boards, 24 inches long.

Procedure: Place each board beside the foot of each lineman so when he pulls, he must step over the board. If he is pulling to trap, the board is

LEAD   TRAP

Diagram 15-3

placed at a 45 degree angle, and if he is pulling to lead block, the board is placed parallel to his foot (see Diagram 15-3). When practicing the short-trap step, the blocker should be aimed directly at the point of attack after he takes the first step. When he is pulling to lead, the first step should permit him to gain depth to clear the wash at the line.

Coaching Points: This drill is designed to break each lineman of the most common mistake when pulling, i.e., of drop-stepping, which results in no progress being made toward the target. The result of this error is obvious. The blocker must take three steps to make one stride toward the target.

Time: This is a five minute introductory drill used during the first week of practice. After the first week this drill is combined with the Board Blocking Drill.

Comments: If a player continues to drop-step when pulling after most of the others have developed this skill, he is given a board to carry with him at all times. Every time he is to pull during dummy scrimmage or signal drill, he will place the board next to his pulling foot. This crutch has worked wonders with many linemen possessed of poor pulling habits.

Short Trap Drill

Equipment: Three stand up dummies for each group.

Procedure: Place three dummies approximately 12 feet to the side of the lineman. One should be placed just beyond the line of scrimmage, another directly on the line and the third about 1 yard in the offensive backfield. The coach should position himself on the far side of the bags facing the puller. See Diagram 15-4. As the blocker takes his second step, the coach will topple the dummy to be blocked. After the trapper has completed the block, he must pick up the bag he has knocked down.

Coaching Points: The object of the drill is to develop quick reactions in your pulling tackles and speed guards. Stress should be placed on short, chopping steps which enable the trapper to have more maneuverability.

Technique: The trapper's initial step is taken at a 45 degree angle to the line of scrimmage. The second step is aimed at the spot where the man to be trapped lines up. By stepping in this manner, the trapper will be in good

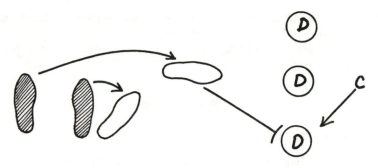

Diagram 15–4

position to block the most difficult type of defender—one that does not penetrate. A penetrating defender presents a much better target to your trapper, who can easily correct his charge to meet this action. The blocker should always make contact with his head in the hole (to the downfield side).

After contact is made, the blocker should continue to drive his feet. Contact is to be made no higher than the waist, and it is important that he follow through in the same fashion used in the fire-block. Many young players will lunge into a trap-block and will end up on the ground with their feet clogging the hole, thus presenting the ballcarrier with an unexpected hazard.

Time: This is a ten-minute drill for ten players spending five minutes blocking in each direction.

Lead Blocking Drill

Equipment: 50 foot rope, large blocking bag, short boards.

Procedure: The puller is to step over the board on his first step, then gain depth prior to entering the track. The track is laid out from the point a ballcarrier would get the ball to the spot downfield where the blocker should intercept a defender, represented by the large blocking bag. The block should be a running shoulder block.

After all the blockers get the idea of running through the bag, a live defender holding a lightweight bag should be substituted for the bag. This player should try to evade the blocker by giving ground, or by taking one step to either side.

Coaching Points: Be sure the defender uses the bag to ward off the block. Occasionally, a defender will attempt to hit the blocker with the bag. This could result in an injury to the defender if he tries to take on the blocker without any protection.

The defender that gives ground on the block is a good test of proper blocking fundamentals. Unless the lead blocker runs through the man using short, chopping steps, a wide base, and waist-high contact, he will not be able to complete the block. But a player that uses these fundamentals properly will snowball a retreating player.

Time: This drill should take ten minutes; five minutes spent going left and five going right.

BACKFIELD PLAY

Center-Quarterback Exchange

Equipment: Chalk circles on the ground showing the positions of the clock, and a large blocking bag for each center.

Procedure: Each quarterback stands in the center of a circle. All of the quarterbacks will take a snap from their center on the cadence of a single quarterback. As the other quarterbacks get the rhythm, they join in calling the snap count. As each center snaps the ball, he is to fire out and block a large dummy placed across the neutral zone. On the snap the quarterback will go through the steps of each series both left and right as directed by the coach. Have the quarterbacks go through the series one step at a time. After they can take the first step properly, have them take two steps, then three, etc. If one of the signal callers makes a mistake, have the whole group repeat the steps. After every few snaps the quarterbacks move to a different center. See Diagram 15-5.

Coaching Points: Stress should be placed on all quarterbacks developing the same cadence with a strong voice inflection. The coach should watch the quarterback's hands to be sure he is placing enough upward

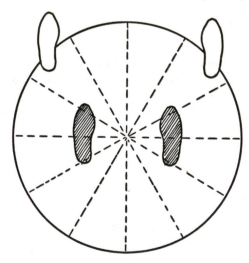

Diagram 15-5

pressure on the center and that he is not pulling out too soon. As the quarterbacks go through their moves, have them stop each time on a designated step and check their feet location on the clock. The players with the poor footwork should be made to note where the quarterbacks with proper footwork are placing their feet.

Time: Five minutes are spent on this drill every day until the first game. Then it is done once a week as a review.

Stance and Starts

Equipment: Chalk 5-yard squares.

Procedure: Have all the fullbacks align one behind the other on a corner of a 5-yard square, with the best in front and the least experienced at the rear. The running backs and swing backs will align in the same order on the squares to either side of the fullbacks. By having the players work in this order, each player can learn from the player ahead of him. Logically, the player to the front is there because he has better technique. The coach positions himself in front of the line to charge and has the players go through the steps of each series in the same step-by-step manner used by the quarterbacks. See Diagram 15–6. The motion procedure is practiced during this drill also. See Diagram 15–7. By having all swing backs or running backs go into motion at the same time, they should all develop the same tempo, which is vital to timing as backs are replaced during a game.

Coaching Points: The coach should place himself at the front of each line as the players make their moves. This position will give him an excellent vantage point to see if any back is out of step. As the backs start, stress should be placed on firing out low and coming up slowly.

Time: Five minutes each day until the first game, then only once a week.

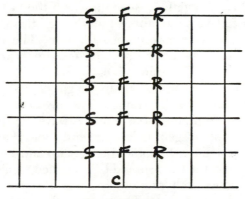

Diagram 15–6

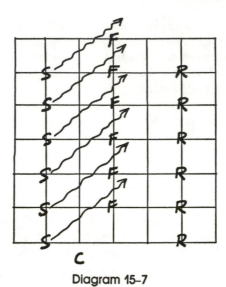

Diagram 15-7

Burma Road Drill

Equipment: Sets of tires, several push-back dummies, and all the large dummies available.

Procedure: The back receives a hand-off and runs through a series of obstacles before reaching the goal line. The obstacles are varied from day to day to keep the drill interesting and challenging.

The first or last obstacle is either a player swinging in baseball fashion a large, lightweight bag at the runner's upper legs, or two defenders standing shoulder to shoulder facing the runner and holding pushbacks for protection. The runner must explode through these barriers to get into the end zone. The other obstacles can be a series of tires, or several prone dummies aligned close together, through which the ballcarrier must step while a gauntlet of players attempt to pull the ball from his grasp or hold bags that are used to create resistance for him. The latter is the most frequently used obstacle because it requires toughness and strength along with good body lean. See Diagram 15-8.

Coaching Points: The bag holders in the gauntlet should be cautioned not to use the bags to club the runner. The pressure on the ballcarrier should come from in front, not from above. Always end the drill at the goal line. Sell the importance of getting into the end zone. If a player falls, send him to the back of the line. Do not let him get up and finish the course. A player that fumbles on the road should be punished, while the runner that scores should be immediately praised.

The drill is tough and tiring. The players who don't have what it takes dislike the drill, while the winners enjoy the challenge. But be they good or bad runners, all learn to fight for every yard. Shortly after we introduced

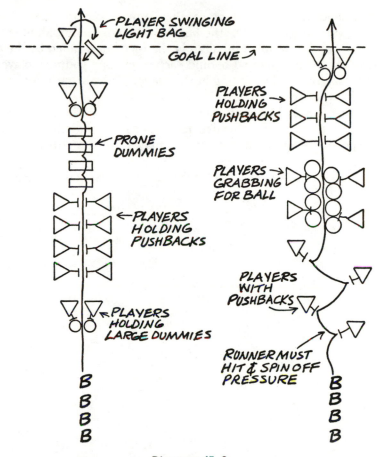

Diagram 15-8

this drill, we noticed backs who normally went down with little resistance become scrappers for that extra yard. Backs that would give up when caught in the pack started breaking through the crowd to make extra yardage. Of all the drills we use, this one is the best for developing tough runners.

Time: Ten minutes every other day all season.

TEAM OFFENSIVE DRILLS

Formations Drill

Formations Drill
Procedure: The head coach should position himself in an elevated location. Below him each offensive unit will align, facing him one behind the other, starting with the best offensive group and working back to the

least experienced. The assistant coaches should spread themselves out among the various groups. On the head coach's command, all of the units will break from the huddle and align in the formation called by the coach. By having the groups aligned behind each other, the younger players can check their alignment by looking at the player in the same position in the group in front of him.

Coaching Points: This is an excellent early season drill to help the team get the total picture of offensive formations. By having the assistant coaches spotted throughout the groups, player adjustments can be made readily.

Time: Five minutes twice a week until the first game, then only as needed.

16

Where Do We Belly From Here?

THE SECRET TO continued success with any offense is its ability to adjust to new defensive trends. If the offense has flexibility and adequate foresight, it need never become dated or outmoded.

No one can accurately predict the future. But by examining the factors that have a bearing on the future, one can draw conclusions based on the trends. Let's delve into the factors acting on the belly.

COACHES

Coaches are certainly more learned today than in any period in the history of the game. Television, literature, clinics, and the like have made knowledge of the game readily available. These avenues of communication have influenced coaching approaches on all levels.

The professional approach to the passing game will soon have its affect on all levels of play, due to the knowledge of the pro game now available.

The pros, especially teams like the San Diego Chargers and Cincinnati Bengals, have made the football field like a large basketball court, with the ball almost always in motion, and quite often by way of the pass. The use of one setback, while enhancing the pass, can be very limiting to a successful ground game. However, this one setback passing approach will eventually send coaches scurrying to find ways to move the ball on the ground. One approach will combine motion with a multi-option approach. This idea seems to blend well with the wide-open passing game.

While quite a few coaches have used triple-option attacks in recent years, only a handful have attempted even greater multiple options (i.e., quad or more options).

Time has been considered the enemy of those coaches interested in multiple option football because the skills necessary for a successful multiple option take so long to develop. Also, the time needed for the staff to develop the understanding of this form of attack have scared off many would-be multiple-option coaches. Finally, most college and high school defenses are geared to stop the run, while pro offenses are built around immobile quarterbacks. These factors are limiting use of the multiple-option attack in today's football.

All of these drawbacks have been solved with the belly option. The offense has continued to be successful over a period of years because of its flexibility. The broad-base attacking theory is always in vogue. By adopting the new forward passing trends, this theory is greatly enhanced by adding depth as well as width to the attack. The authors may be somewhat prejudiced, but the results do speak for themselves. Consequently, the belly option is not only an offense for today but for the future as well.

PLAYERS

The improvement of the young men playing the game is certainly another factor that will have a bearing on the future of belly option football.

Much of your success depends upon the interest of the young men operating the offense. This interest leads to skill people working on their skills in the off-season. This has long been considered illegal; in fact, not only has the idea of off-season workout been frowned upon, it has often been legislated against. Imagine stopping a musician from practicing all year round! But today the courts are stepping in to prevent such legislation.

Today, skill position players are getting more chances to participate in touch seven-on-seven games in the off-season. By so doing, they are raising their ball skills (passing, catching, running, etc.) to a much higher efficiency level.

The idea started in the Sunbelt States. The "passing leagues" formulated in California have provided off-season opportunities for high school players to sharpen their passing game skills, and the results can be seen by the number of outstanding passers and receivers flooding the college ranks from that region of our country. The potentiality can be seen by anyone with a bit of imagination. By using some of the large indoor facilities available throughout the country, this idea will be instituted in the winter as well. Future football players will have the chance to hone their game year-round, not just in the three- or four-month season now available.

RULES

The playing rules certainly have a bearing on how the game is played. The use of the hands in blocking, especially pass-blocking, in pro and college football, makes it advantageous to incorporate the pass as the main way of moving the ball. On the other hand, the limits placed on run game blocking at the high school level will doubtless lead to a more wide-open game. Again, the belly option comes to mind when a coach looks for a ground game that mixes easily with increased emphasis on the pass.

Let's examine the direct influence these factors have on the belly option.

The broad based frontal attack of the belly blends well with the pass-oriented, depth attack of the one-back set when combined with the multiple formation possibilities (see Diagrams 16–1 and 16–2 for examples).

As you can see, the belly theory still provides multiple points of attack along the front that many other offenses would lack with only one setback.

The coach who is still not ready to make the complete transition to the passing game with a one-back set can still use most of the advantages of the wide-open passing game while maintaining a two-back set. By using multiple two-back formations along with motion and/or shifting, the essentials of the passing game can be implemented while still retaining the basic belly option offense (see Diagrams 16–3 and 16–4).

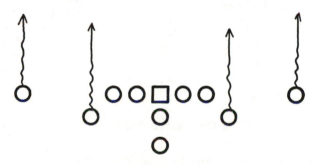

Diagram 16–1

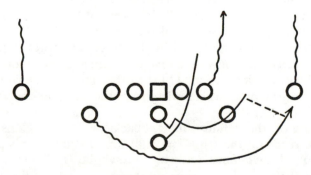

Diagram 16–2

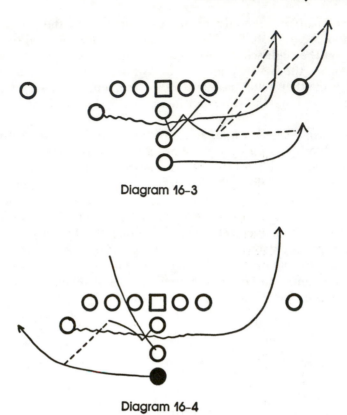

Diagram 16-3

Diagram 16-4

FUTURE OFFENSIVE PHILOSOPHY

Open your mind to see the possibilities; come with us for a look at what could be the offense of the future: a combination of a professional passing game and a multiple-option belly offense geared to the flexibility of current basketball offenses. The quarterback in the multi-option has over four options. He can give to the fullback, keep it himself, pitch it to the trailing back, or pass to any of several receivers.

His first decision is determined by the defense's approach to the dive play. If the quarterback believes the dive back can gain 4 or more yards on the handoff, he gives him the ball. On the other hand, if the running lane appears jammed, the quarterback withdraws the ball and checks his pass read.

Depending on the defense, the fullback has three options after the handoff as he reads on the run. The fullback can stay on his patch and accelerate, or read the defense and run to daylight. If his dive path is not threatened from the inside, outside, or straight on by the linebacker, he accelerates. If the nose guard attacks his path, the fullback veers back over the center. On the other hand, if the defensive tackle pinches inside, the diveback cuts outside into the seam outside the offensive tackle.

If the quarterback pitches to the tailback, he has two options at his disposal: He can continue to run with the pitch, or he can pass on the run to any of several receivers.

Earlier it was mentioned that the quarterback has over four options. The extra options come from using the other receivers in addition to the onside, inside receiver. Two possibilities are the slat of short post to the onside wide receiver or the same pattern to the offside wide receiver.

His run-or-pass decision is based on the secondaries reaction. If a defensive back starts to attack the pitch, the pass is the choice. If no pressure is placed on the pitch, the tailback can turn the corner for a big gain.

It should be noted that the receivers change their course after the ball is pitched to the tailback, as shown in Diagram 16-5. This allows the receivers to be in position to receive a pass from the tailback.

The passing routes shown in Diagrams 16-6a and 16-6b show another attacking method: the reading pass routes. This idea comes in two distinct variations. The first idea is for the receiver to read the defensive secondary coverages. The receiver makes his cut according to the coverage. The quarterback also reads the coverage and passes to the receiver when he reaches his final cut. On his release, the split end reads the basic invert zone and runs his sideline route. The quarterback also reads the coverage and delivers the pass to the split end when the latter makes his final cut (see Diagram 16-6a). Diagram 16-6b shows another read variation versus the secondary using the five-under, two-deep zone coverage. The split end reads the coverage and runs a fade or flat route. The quarterback follows suit and delivers on the long route.

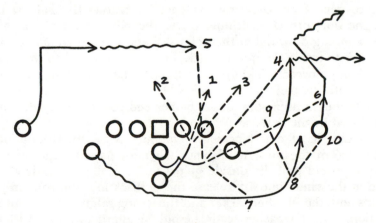

Diagram 16-5

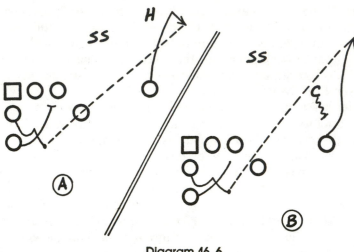

Diagram 16-6

The second read approach has the receivers running predetermined routes. The quarterback reads the coverage and passes to the open receiver (see Diagram 16-5). Both of these read approaches have proven successful. Imagine the potential of a combination of the read routes with the multi-option!

For example, in the fifty-two Oklahoma defense, the onside linebacker will be the initial key to both the give and the arc pass. Assuming the backer honors the dive, the quarterback knows this defender will not bother the arc pattern. This approach usually puts a dual-responsibility burden on the strong safety or the weakside cornerback, depending on the direction of the play. The quarterback straightens up after the short-belly ride and looks at the receiver running the arc. If the strong safety (or weakside corner) is not covering the pass, he throws the ball. If he is covered, the quarterback continues on to the next phase of the multi-option by running downhill at the defensive end's inside shoulder. If the end prepares to tackle the quarterback, he pitches the ball to the trailing back; if the end moves upfield to stop the pitch, the quarterback continues on his path with the ball.

Also, add in multiple-blocking schemes and you get some idea of the problems faced by the defense.

One example of new blocking techniques is to run the option by combining two of the present blocking schemes. As is normal with this offense, you would pull the onside guard to block the frontside contain man, and at the same time arc-release the slotback into the contain man. This places both the fifty linebacker and the strong safety in a very precarious position. If the linebacker reads the pulling guard and flows with him, the quarterback gives the fullback the ball. If he fills, the quarterback will read the strong safety for an arc pass or pitch (see Diagram 16-7).

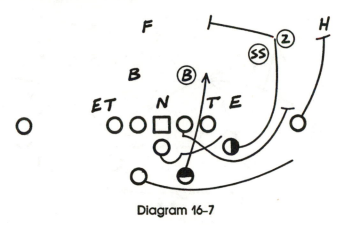

Diagram 16–7

Certainly the wrong decision can be made by any of the offensive operators; but, as in basketball, by repetition the multiple-choice potential of the offense should be right much more than it is wrong.

If your skilled people are inexperienced, you could threaten all of the options on any snap but predetermine the use of one or two choices in the huddle. This creates a guessing game, but the defense still has to concern themselves with the potential of all the options. The major advantage of this plan would lessen the risk of turnovers, which is certainly a vital consideration.

In addition to those plays already discussed, it is anticipated that other plays will also be a part of the belly option arsenal. The shotgun influence will probably be felt by the belly option also. The passing success of the Dallas Cowboys and other pro teams when operating in the shotgun gives you a glimpse of the shotgun and belly option potential. College teams, such as Wichita State, have used the shotgun as a running-game weapon. Their shotgun has gained renown in coaching circles. How can this fit into the belly's future?

By aligning in a shotgun, the threat of a pass unhampered by blitzes is always imminent. By splitting both ends and showing a slotback on either side, the pass or option threat could develop quickly. If the remaining set back is aligned in either slot, the defense faces a real challenge. Five primary receivers can force any defense to loosen up considerably (see Diagrams 16–8 and 16–9). Two minor technique adjustments can start a belly series so quickly that the defense would not have time to convert from pass to run. If the three slotbacks align at a depth of 3 yards, one could motion back to the fullback slot in just three quick steps, providing the quarterback with the inside running threat. The slotback to the side of the option need not come all the way across the backfield to become a pitchback threat.

We have been using a pitchback turnaround motion for several years with no problem. But by placing the diveback in motion, the pitchback is denied the opportunity to position himself behind the quarterback. To

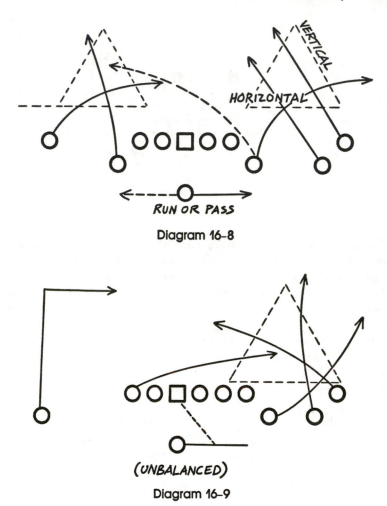

Diagram 16-8

Diagram 16-9

(UNBALANCED)

compensate for this, he must get into the running lane prior to the pitch point as shown in Diagrams 16–10 and 16–11. If there really are backs that can be at top speed in two or three steps, a short move in and a turnaround should prove no trouble.

All the same rules still apply for determining run or pass, inside or outside, and left or right. It's an idea soon to come. This approach would cause the defense to defend the entire field from sideline to sideline and from the line of scrimmage to the goal line on every snap. The pass threat would keep deep defenders playing loose until it is too late to be effective run supporters. The linebackers would be forced to defend a player skilled enough to catch the pass or run from the option. The front defenders would have to be able to play pass or run on virtually every down. Con-

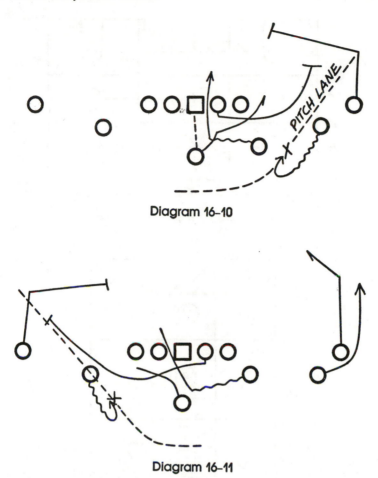

Diagram 16-10

Diagram 16-11

sequently, defensive football coaches would have to develop an approach similar to that used in basketball, but with an attack area three to 12 times as large, depending on vertical field position (see Diagrams 16–12 and 16–13).

Imagine playing basketball defense on a court at least three times the current standard size (90′ × 50′), and you will get some idea of the task facing defensive coordinators in the future. The possibility of a position player getting one-on-one with any defender in an open field is an offensive coach's dream. The multiple option discussed here will present this opportunity on almost every snap of the ball.

Fifty years ago, 100 points by a team in basketball would have been considered impossible. Today it is commonplace. Take the theories discussed here and 60 to 75 points per game by a football offense could be a regular occurrence, not just a freakish blow-out performance. Conces-

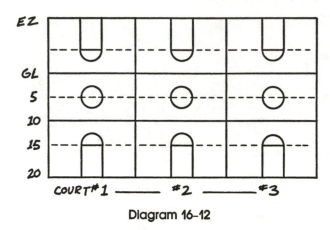

Diagram 16-12

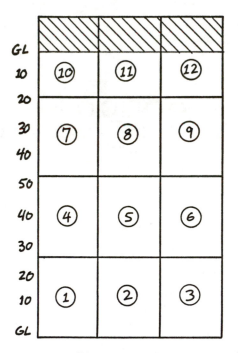

Diagram 16-13

sionaires might not like this because spectators would be too busy enjoying offensive football to leave their seats for a trip to the concession counter.

This will require offensive coaches to re-adjust their thinking regarding scoring potential. It has always been assumed that a high-scoring offense would score an average of five times a game on an average of 13 possessions. This theory means that on eight occasions the offense will not score. Why does this ratio permeate our thinking? There are two reasons: one is that the offense will stop itself, and the other is that the defense is considered stronger than the offense.

What will be required to change these negative offensive facts? For one, as offensive skill people work to develop their skills in the off-season (as basketball players have been doing over the last 25 years), the offensive will stop themselves less frequently. For another, the multiple-option theory previously discussed will limit the defense's ability to gang up on offense as they do to some attacks today. Just one more scoring possession coupled with one more defensive breakdown would result in two more scores per game. Therefore, a high-scoring machine of today (35 points or five scores) could score seven touchdowns in the future. That's offensive production! And it is certainly a goal within reach.

There is a precedent for this type of thinking. Just look at Diagram 16–14 and compare the NCAA scoring statistics over the period from 1937 to 1980. Despite drops in team scoring by both teams at two intervals, the trend is still toward increased scoring; in fact, scoring has actually doubled since the NCAA started keeping stats in 1937. This production has come with only a few of the concepts discussed in this chapter.

NCAA - TWO TEAM SCORING	
1937 —— 20.2	1960 —— 31.1 (ONE PLATOON)
1940 —— 26.6	1970 —— 42.6
1950 —— 37.8	1980 —— 41.0

Diagram 16–14

Index